What People Are Saying
and *The Power of God*

With the skill of a teacher and the _____ a forerunner, Ray McCollum releases the spirit _____ ...dom and revelation in his life-altering book on a God-given imagination. You need this!

—*Dr. James W. Goll*
Encounters Network
International best-selling author

In an era where we are all in need of encouragement, inspiration, and hope, I commend Ray McCollum's book with a double thumbs up! Tackling an easily misunderstood theme, the author delivers material that is well-balanced and well-written. Read it and release those dreams God has put in your heart!

—*Larry Tomczak*
Larry Tomczak Ministries

Ray McCollum has written something beyond a "really important book"; he has written a seminal book, a book capable of seeding real change. Very few concepts are more important than faith coupled with foreseen vision. This is what Ray has re-opened for many of us, the truth that eternal reality is birthed, matured, and released from its imagined reality within us. Pray as you read and may Christ re-open what may have been closed within you!

—*Dennis Peacocke*
Founder and president of GoStrategic
(formerly Strategic Christian Services)

Everything I have been privileged to witness in the life and ministry of Ray McCollum over the last twenty years is on display in this powerful new book: clarity, vision, leadership, steadfastness, courage, faithfulness, and creativity. It really is must-reading for anyone and everyone who would dare to dream of a better day and a better way.

—*Dr. George Grant*
Pastor of Parish Presbyterian Church
Franklin, TN
Founder of New College Franklin and Franklin Classical School
President of the King's Meadow Study Center

This book by Ray McCollum is a key that, when used, unlocks one of the most powerful aspects of our inner being, our God-given imagination. Through this manuscript, Ray functions as a master facilitator and a helpful enabler whose goal is to support the readers as they pursue their objectives. My hope is that you will get as "stoked" as I was from breathing in this treasure trove of inspiration. May all your dreams come true as you release your creativity.

—*Mickey Robinson*
International speaker
Author, *Heaven*
Co-founder of Prophetic Destiny International

John Milton wrote, "I am not afraid of falsehood entering into the marketplace of ideas as long as truth is presented because truth will always prevail." Ray McCollum's book, *The Power of God-Given Imagination*, gives a vivid picture of amazing truth prevailing against a plethora of falsehoods plaguing mankind. This book is a deep well of revelation and activation for living according to our God-given design. It will inspire, challenge, and equip you. I have known Ray for many years, and I wholeheartedly recommend this book to anyone hungry for something better.

—*Dr. Bill Bennot*
President of BMosaic
Senior pastor, Journey of Grace, Cape Town, South Africa

Ray McCollum has emphasized a subject that has been largely ignored or castigated as New Age thinking. He has made the subject of imagination easy to understand and shows how it affects our everyday life. Someone once said, "Intelligence is not a sign of knowledge but of imagination." I am so glad that Ray has chosen to write about our God-given ability to imagine—and how to use that ability correctly!

—*Pastor Kerry Kirkwood*
Author, *The Power of Imagination*

As I savored the pages of Ray's book I found myself experiencing not only inspiration to dream but also an unexpected impartation. I marveled at feeling my own dreams coming alive and gaining fresh momentum in the theater of my imagination. From my experience with Ray McCollum as a man of quality character and deeds, and through my own encounter with the power of this book, I highly recommend this timely and compelling read.

—*Dan McCollam*
Author and international director of Sounds of the Nations

Few Christians understand how to use their God-given imagination. Ray has done a masterful job of revealing the power of imagination and how to use it for the glory of God. I believe this book should be required reading for every Christian!

—*Happy Caldwell*
Founder and president, Victory Television Network
Author, *Unleashing Heaven's Blessings*

If you've ever looked into the eyes of a child, you have seen the sparkle of imagination. Yet, as we age, our hearts begin to dull to imaginary things and we methodically lumber through life on a steady diet of the ordinary. But we can be born again! This is the gospel message! Ray McCollum shows us in fresh and sensible ways that God has given the gift of imagination to each one of us—and it was never intended to fade away. Read this book, and just imagine....

—*James Ryle*
Author, *Hippo in the Garden* and *A Dream Come True*

The
Power of God-Given
IMAGINATION

RAY McCOLLUM

WHITAKER
HOUSE

Boldface type in the Scripture quotations indicates the author's emphasis.
Unless otherwise indicated, all dictionary definitions are taken from *Dictionary.com Unabridged*, Random House, © 2015.

The Power of God-Given Imagination:
Releasing the Power Within You to Transform the World Around You
www.pastorray.com • ray@pastorray.com

ISBN: 978-1-62911-5542 • eBook ISBN: 978-1-62911-5764
Printed in the United States of America
© 2015 by Ray W. McCollum

Whitaker House
1030 Hunt Valley Circle
New Kensington, PA 15068
www.whitakerhouse.com

Library of Congress Cataloging-in-Publication Data

McCollum, Ray W., 1944–
  The power of God-given imagination : releasing the power within you to transform the world around you / by Ray W. McCollum. — First [edition].
    pages cm
  Summary: "Ray McCollum challenges the Christian reader to reclaim the power of imagination, so often used for success only in the business or self-help world, and to instead use it to unlock a future of hope, blessing, and answered prayer"— Provided by publisher.
  ISBN 978-1-62911-554-2 (trade pbk. : alk. paper) — ISBN 978-1-62911-576-4 (ebook) 1. Imagination—Religious aspects—Christianity. I. Title.
  BR115.I6M33 2015
  233'.5—dc23
                    2015031897

1 2 3 4 5 6 7 8 9 10 11 ⨆ 22 21 20 19 18 17 16 15

To Ted L. Snider

I went to work for Ted L. Snider in 1975, just four years after my conversion to Christ. Ted was a true "imagineer" and an amazing mentor to me. He was a model of what Christian leadership in the corporate world ought to look like. I will be eternally grateful for all that I learned during the seven years I worked for him, lessons that helped me better serve God's people during the my past thirty-two years of pastoral ministry.

God bless you, Ted.

TABLE OF CONTENTS

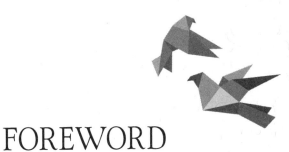

FOREWORD

Consider the words of the great poet, Langston Hughes:

> ...if dreams die
> Life is a broken-winged bird
> That cannot fly.
> ...when dreams go
> Life is a barren field
> Frozen with snow.[1]

The first revelation we have of God in the Scripture is that God is the Creator. This Creator had a clear and lucid dream of what His creation would look like when He began. While the artist always begins with a blank canvas, the artist never begins without an idea in her or his imagination of what is to be articulated on that canvas. Most great artists know the "end from the beginning," even

---

1. Langston Hughes, *The Collected Works of Langston Hughes: Works for Children and Young Adults: Poetry, Fiction, and Other Writing*, vol. 11 (Columbia, MO: University of Missouri Press, 2003), 52.

as most architects build the structures in their imaginations long before the buildings are ever are constructed in reality.

This One who dreamed and created the world through six successive stages in three realms to build a three-tiered universe, a three-storied cosmic house, is the Divine Artist. Andrew Jukes tells of the creative process God manifests in the stages of creation by saying that the first three days were days of *bounding and dividing*, separating out three realms from each other, and the last three days were spent by God *furnishing and adorning* the three realms He had bounded and divided.

He culminates His artistic and imaginative handiwork by stooping down to the ground and getting His hands in its "dust." *Dust* is used in Hebrew for our idea of "debris," interestingly enough, implying decomposition.

So God gets His hands "dirty" with the organic components of the soil, formed by the decomposition of leaves and other plant materials by the unseen microscopic microorganisms that tell the gospel story in their own life journey of death, burial, and resurrection. The soil, the "dust," is what scientists call "humus," from which God forms the first "human" being, in His *image* and *likeness*.

God then takes the human He has formed and places him in a rich, luxurious, cultivated place and invites him to dream. Here the human being is to continue to dream God's dream, and cultivate and protect what is there from the untamed wild things that could intrude on it.

Being a husbandman, a tiller of the soil, of the raw material from which Adam came, required not only the labor of his hands, it required the exercise of his imagination. Keeping Paradise looking like Paradise required an eye for aesthetics, an eye for beauty, an eye for detail, an eye for depth, color coordination, placement, and all the rest. It required artistry and creativity. In other words, it required a sensory-rich imagination.

The Creator God had imagined the world He created, and then, from that amazing, architecturally rich and fertile divine imagination, filled with the substance of His desire, He spoke and made manifest what His imagination conceived. God cultivated what He conceived in His imagination.

So too, the creative process in the human experience is inseparable from the conceptions of the imagination. It takes a dreaming mind to fuel the flames of the creative process.

Adam was "placed" in a pristine, sensory-rich environment filled with the brightest of colors, the widest spectrum of textures, and the optimal environment for the awakening of his spiritual and physical senses to their highest and greatest potential. For what purpose, you might ask? To take the raw material of that glorious paradisiacal garden and use it to build a habitation for God's glory to cover the earth as the waters cover the sea.

Sadly, Adam's opportunity to cultivate God's dream in Paradise ended due to the choice he made to be independent of the Creator, failing to protect what God had created. Adam bought into the beastly deception of "copying" and "counterfeiting," thereby co-opting the opportunity for dreaming and experiencing life as a nightmare instead. When Adam "died" after eating the forbidden fruit, he did not yet draw his last breath, but he did lose his spiritual sight, from which all great dreams emerge. Dead men cannot see.

In the New Creation, Jesus takes the same dust we came from, and spits on it, and places two mud-balls with His DNA saturating it, into the empty eye-sockets of a man born blind. Jesus then tells him to go to a pool called "Sent" (Siloam), where he is "apostle-ized" (to be sent) to *wash* his eye-sockets now filled with anointed mud-balls and then *see* what happens when God works the kind of works that we were born to dream about and then do with Him.

All of us are "the man born blind" outside of Christ; all of us need Him to spit on the dust of our fallen and broken humanity and give us new eyes to see and dream with God again. We need our spiritual sight recovered and restored so that we can dream with God.

From a neurological perspective, that man born blind had no idea what it was like to see. However, he certainly had the ability, the God-given ability, to dream about it. Scientists have demonstrated that the thoughts that show up in the so-called "mental workspace" of our brain alter our perceptions of reality. In other words, imagination affects how we see and how we hear. The man who was born blind, however, couldn't dream about what it was like to see because his imagination hadn't experienced it—it had only experienced the sense of hearing.

The disciples spoke to Jesus in the presence of the man born blind as if he were also deaf, even though he could hear quite well. They had no regard for his feelings when they gave voice to a common yet false assumption, *"Who sinned, this man or his parents, that he would be born blind?"* (John 9:2). The residue of those words could easily have killed the man's hopes or abilities to dream beyond his blindness.

The Master Dreamer quickly nullified their folly and reassured the listening blind man that God still held out for a dream for him to see. When Jesus speaks, faith comes. When faith comes, imagination awakens, dreams are revived, and vision comes to pass. Jesus said, "*Neither...this man sinned, nor his parents*" (verse 3). What a comfort to that man's ears and heart! This wasn't his "fault." Jesus didn't stop there; He primed the pump of imagination and said that His Father set this whole thing up so that the wonderful works of His Father could be manifest in the man. This man was about to gain something he had never had: the ability to *see*!

Real creativity is the stuff of an imagination rooted and grounded in the Creator's inspiring impulses, surging through the depths of the human spirit and the lens of a sanctified imagination, and then clothed with words and actions equal to the vision inspired by the breath of God. In Job we hear these words: "*It is a spirit in man, and the breath of the Almighty gives them understanding*" (Job 32:8).

The anointing of God, the DNA of God's saliva, on the dust of our disappointments, enables us to regain our sight so we can *see* what we have been missing in life.

If ever we needed God to "spit" on the curses in the dust of our own broken dreams, it is today. It is in the dust of former dreams long forgotten, that the potential for new dreams rise because our dust "remembers." Memory, imagination, possibility, faith, hope, and resilience...this is the "stuff" from which dreams are made.

In the following pages, Ray McCollum takes you on an amazing journey of awakening the as-yet-dormant potential lying in the dust of your disappointments. He explains that God doesn't want to just fulfill a dream for you; He wants to fulfill a dream in you and with you! When the way you see who you are changes, the world around you will change. Dreaming dreams is healthy. A God-given, sanctified imagination isn't an option in life; it is a necessity. *The Power of a God-Given Imagination* is a grace gift to empower you from the inside-out to *see* what you have been missing, so you can work the works of Him who sent you.

Drink deeply from the well that Ray McCollum has dug for you from the soil of the greatest story ever told, and start seeing what God intends to do for you, with you, and through you!

—*Bishop Mark J. Chironna, MA, PhD*
Mark Chironna Ministries
Church On The Living Edge
Orlando, Florida

INTRODUCTION: AWAKENING THE DREAMER WITHIN YOU

Sometimes the secular "prophets" say it better than the church. Singer/songwriter Carly Simon's song "Let the River Run," which plays in the opening credits of the 1988 film *Working Girl,* gets it right when it calls for "dreamers" to "wake the nation." But who will awaken the dreamers?

This book is about awakening the dreamer within *you.* In these pages, you will learn how to become an "imagineer," using the power *within* you to transform the world *around* you.

Basic Instincts

All human beings are hardwired with certain basic instincts. These inborn patterns, or tendencies, are unlearned. We come by them naturally. These strong inner desires compel us to love, procreate, and even cover our ears at rock concerts.

The most basic human instinct is survival. In any given situation, we will do whatever it takes to stay alive. Lifeguards know that a drowning swimmer will do anything to save himself—even drown his rescuer! No one has to teach us how to protect ourselves from a perceived danger because the will to survive is present in all of us from birth. It's an instinct—something we do quite naturally.

But there is another basic instinct all humans share that's often overlooked. This book is about *that* instinct—our inborn predisposition to imagine, to envision, and to dream.

Even when marred and disfigured by sin, the human soul cries out from within for a better world and a better life. Something deep inside us simply refuses to accept life's bitter drink. We push forward, day by day, dealing with the challenges and difficulties of life as best we can. We don't give up, because, instinctively, we believe there is more to life than what we are experiencing. The hopes and dreams within us are like iron filings being pulled toward the magnet of a "preferred" future, a better life for ourselves and a better world for those we care about.

Awakening the Dreamers Who Will Awaken the Nation

Those hopes and dreams can inspire others, as well. Dreamers really *do* awake the nation.

In fact, they already *have*. Let me give you an example that hits close to home. Our nation was founded by dreamers. History shows that our forefathers dreamed of a "New Jerusalem," a "city set on a hill," and imagined that it would be a demonstration of the kingdom of God on earth.

Most of the nations of the earth evolved out of people groups that eventually set geographical boundaries and developed their distinct identity over a long period of time. Not America. We are a nation "born in a day," the product of the imagination of a group of diverse men who came together to make their dream come true. And on July 4, 1776, it did.

But over the years, our nation has strayed away from the dream many times. The issue of slavery took America into a bloody, four-year Civil War. A few months after one of the deadliest exchanges, the Battle of Gettysburg, President Abraham Lincoln rose to speak at the dedication of the Soldiers' National Cemetery in Gettysburg, Pennsylvania. His famous Gettysburg Address is still one of the best-known speeches in American history. He only spoke ten sentences for just over two minutes. So what made this brief speech so famous? Why was it so effective? Consider the opening lines:

> Four score and seven years ago our fathers brought forth on this continent, a new nation, conceived in liberty, and dedicated to the proposition that all men are created equal.[2]

The power of President Lincoln's speech lay in his ability to reawaken the nation to the original dream of its founders. Many had forgotten who they were; he was reminding them of the original dream.

In the closing lines of his speech, Lincoln calls Americans to a "new birth" as the people their fathers had imagined them to be.

---

2. Abraham Lincoln, "Gettysburg Address", November 19, 1863, Abraham Lincoln Online, http://www.abrahamlincolnonline.org/lincoln/speeches/gettysburg.htm. Lincoln delivered this speech during the American Civil War at the dedication of the Soldiers' National Cemetery in Gettysburg, Pennsylvania.

...that from these honored dead we take increased devotion to that cause for which they gave the last full measure of devotion—that we here highly resolve that these dead shall not have died in vain—*that this nation, under God, shall have a new birth of freedom—and that government of the people, by the people, for the people, shall not perish from the earth.*[3]

This would not be the last time that God would use a dreamer to awaken the nation.

The Civil War ended with the abolition of slavery. But the problem of racial inequality and prejudice continued, boiling over into the 1950s and 1960s. In 1863, God used Abraham Lincoln to awaken Americans to the American Dream. Almost exactly one hundred years later, in 1963, God raised up another dreamer to reawaken us to the noble message of equality among men. His name was Martin Luther King, Jr. Like Lincoln, he delivered one of the most famous speeches in American history. His message was simple but profound:

I have a dream that my four little children will one day live in a nation where they will not be judged by the color of their skin but by the content of their character.[4]

Dr. King was a dreamer who refused to accept things as they were. He *imagined* a better future and put it into words that inspire us to this day. The speech resonated with everyone, black and white, and the picture he painted was of a nation in which men were measured by the content of their character instead of the color of their skin. Dr. King was assassinated, but the images he painted with his words will live on forever.

3. Ibid., emphasis added.
4. Martin Luther King Jr., "I Have a Dream," August 28, 1963, American Rhetoric, http://www.americanrhetoric.com/speeches/mlkihaveadream.htm.

Great leaders like President Lincoln and Dr. King are always great dreamers. They are not engineers; they are "imagineers," a term coined by Walt Disney for his creative team members. Great men are great because they imagine great things. They refuse to accept the status quo. They always believe things can be better. Robert F. Kennedy said, "There are those who look at things the way they are, and ask *why?* I dream of things that never were, and ask *why not?*"

Not everyone is called to change nations. But even the most ordinary person among us can tap into the power of imagination, using the power *within* us to change the world *around* us.

My Dad, the Dreamer

My dear father passed away in 1996. He was not a churchman, and did not teach me Christ. But he will always hold a place in my heart for the many good things that he modeled. Dad came from lower middle-class Irish stock. His mother deserted his family when he was little, and his father struggled with alcohol, so he and his sister ended up in foster home in New Orleans. He finished only fourth grade and left home to join the Marine Corps at age seventeen (to get in, he lied about his age).

When he married my mom, he was a mortician's assistant at a funeral home. They lived above the mortuary for a while, but Mom made him look for another job because she couldn't stand the smell of the embalming fluids. Dad went on to become a motorcycle cop in Victoria, Texas.

When I was born in 1944, he was working as a brakeman for the Southern Pacific Railroad, and in 1952, he bought a Texaco service station in Lake Charles, Louisiana, and moved our family there. (In those days, nobody pumped their own gas.) Dad left the house before sunrise every day, and Mom would prepare a hot lunch for him that we would deliver daily. He worked 60–70 hours a week, six days a week, and rarely got home before 6 PM. My most indelible impression of my Father growing up was how hard he worked! When I hear the term "strong work ethic," I always think of my dad.

It wasn't until after his death that I came to understand the *source* of his work ethic. My dad was a dreamer. He tapped into the awesome power of the American sociology, or "ethos."

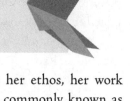

Ethos: the fundamental character or spirit of a culture; the underlying sentiment that informs the beliefs, customs, or practices of a group or society; dominant assumptions of a people.

The secret of America's greatness is her ethos, her work ethic, and her citizens' pursuit, which is commonly known as the American Dream.

The American Dream

The birth of our nation was conceived, or imagined, by our founding fathers, and the American Dream is their legacy to us.

[The American Dream is] that dream of a land in which life should be better and richer and fuller for everyone, with opportunity for each according to ability or achievement…. It is not a dream of motor cars and high wages merely, but a dream of social order in which each man and

each woman shall be able to attain to the fullest stature
of which they are innately capable, and be recognized by
others for what they are, regardless of the fortuitous circumstances of birth or position.[5]

America is truly exceptional. Yet no nation, not even ours,
is perfect. I am not here to idealize the American Dream. But it
is important for us to see how the imagination and the dreams
of our forefathers created an environment for every generation
that followed. For example, I now realize that my dad's faith in
the American Dream was the power source of his amazing work
ethic. He made up for his lack of formal education and financial
advantage by simply *outworking* everybody else. He had many
setbacks, but, eventually, in his late 60s, he started a railroad
maintenance company, doing contract work at the rail yards
for the oil refineries in the Lake Charles area. He didn't make
a million dollars, but he paid off the mortgage on our home and
died debt-free at age eighty-two. My father carried the American
Dream inside himself, and there was enough power in it to keep
him going until it all came true.

Dad imparted that same spirit to me. I did not have a silver
spoon in my mouth, wealthy relatives, a college degree, or any-
body rich and powerful to help me. But I never really considered myself disadvantaged. I always believed that I could succeed
in life by being the best at whatever I set my mind to do, and
I always seemed to have the energy and the pluck to outwork
everybody else.

It was only after I came to Christ in 1971 that the Lord
began to show me how my boyhood dreams and imaginations
of future success were providing the power that helped me to get

5. James Truslow Adams, *The Epic of America* (Boston: Little, Brown, and Co.,
1931), 214–215.

there. Unfortunately, succeeding generations are being weaned away from the original dream (freedom to work hard and succeed by taking personal responsibility for one's situation) and are instead being seduced into believing that it's the federal government's job to make sure that they are happy and well taken care of. This new dream offers us security and well-being as an entitlement, whereas the original American Dream offered only the opportunity for life, liberty, and the pursuit of happiness. We need a national reawakening that restores the principles that made us great.

Who Will Awaken the Dreamers?

I love America. The freedom our citizens have to hope, dream, and work to create a better life for themselves has been an inspiration that people and governments around the world still strive to emulate. But our nation is in trouble. The foundational values that made us great are under attack. We are in a moral free fall, and far too many of our young people seem uninspired or frustrated that the Dream is no longer available to them. Even the secular statisticians recognize this to be the problem. Blogger Kimberly Amadeo comments:

> Even before the recession, most Americans had lost hope in the [American] Dream. A 2004 survey found that two-thirds felt the Dream was becoming harder to achieve, especially for young families. They named financial insecurity, poor quality education and even the government itself as the worst barriers. More than 30% felt they weren't living the Dream, and nearly half thought it was unattainable for them.[6]

6. Kimberly Amadeo, "The End of the American Dream: Is the American Dream Still Alive?" http://useconomy.about.com/od/grossdomesticproduct/a/American_Dream.htm.

The human heart abhors a "dream vacuum." Our Christian forefathers imagined America to be a New Jerusalem, a city set on a hill, and a demonstration of the kingdom of God on earth. The power of those dreams gave birth to our nation and made her great. But if that dream dies, the human heart will demand that it be replaced by another dream.

President Barack Obama was elected twice on a platform of hope and change. The message of hope always resonates within us, because hope is the oxygen of the soul. Theologian Emil Brunner explained the importance of hope with these words: "What oxygen is to the lungs, such is hope to the meaning of life." President Obama's message of "hope" got him elected twice. For some, however, it seems as though the change has led to nothing more than an enlargement of the federal government's role in individual lives. I fear that a growing number of Americans, especially non-Christians and young people, seem to be willing to give up their personal freedoms in exchange for the cradle-to-the-grave security being promised by an increasingly powerful centralized government. This sort of imagination is called "statism."

Statism: the principle or policy of concentrating extensive economic, political, and related controls in the state at the cost of individual liberty.

Notice that there are two irreconcilable transcendences in this definition: control by the state and individual liberty. The American Dream idealizes individual liberty, while statism presumes control by the state. The foundational philosophies behind these two dreams are clearly presented in the Scriptures in the following two cities: Babylon, the city of man, and Jerusalem, the city of God. These two philosophies are irreconcilable and mutually exclusive. They are now, and have always been, at war with each other. There is power in both because each imagines a future. Which dream will prevail?

Whether she knows it or not, Carly Simon got it right. We need dreamers to reawaken the nation to God's goal—the New Jerusalem, or God's kingdom *"on earth as it is in heaven"* (Matthew 6:10 niv).

This is not a political book. I'm simply using political imagery to illustrate the power of inner images to shape our future. Communism, socialism, and statism have never worked anywhere, anytime. These systems fail because they suppress people's freedom to dream, imagine, and creatively invent things that will make life better for everyone. The greatest advancements in human history have come from America and other nations where individual liberty is valued and protected. The pollsters tell us that the majority of Americans today do not believe life will be as good for their children and grandchildren as it was for them. Pessimism reigns. But it's not too late. When God's dreamers wake up, they can awake the nation.

Your Part to Play

As a pastor, I am grieved to see the church of Jesus Christ so marginalized and ineffective in our deteriorating culture. As a father and a grandfather, I am deeply concerned about the future of my children and grandchildren. As an American, I am troubled by what's going on in Washington.

On the other hand, my faith for another great awakening has never been higher. I am not looking for salvation from politicians, "super pastors," or world systems. I am looking for God to raise up a new generation of dreamers to awaken the nation. I'm expecting it to begin with an awakening of the people of God—His precious church. I'm talking about *you*!

This book is about discovering the power *within* you—the power to dream, envision, and *imagine*—to change the world around you. This power is so God-like that, out of all the creation, it is only bestowed on men and women who are made in the *image* and likeness of God Himself. (See Genesis 1:27.)

Within the pages of this book, you will discover exactly what this power is, how it works, and how you can use it to transform your personal life and to release the kingdom of God to transform the culture around you.

This is the power of God-given imagination!

—*Ray McCollum*

1

GOD'S AMAZING GIFT
TO MANKIND

Our nation was founded on the principle that "all men are created equal," meaning that every human being has intrinsic value in the sight of God and is entitled to "certain inalienable Rights."[7]

On the other hand, all men are definitely not created equal when it comes to gifts, talents, and abilities. We don't get past third grade without learning that some people are just plain smarter than we are, and we learn on the playground that some can run faster than we can. As we get older, we discover that we have our own special "sweet spots." We may notice that others surpass us in math or that we have a special knack for literature. It is an ontological fact that all men are created equal. But it's a discernible fact that *not* all men and women are gifted equally.

---

7. Thomas Jefferson, "The Declaration of Independence," *Historic American Documents*, Lit2Go Edition, (1776), http://www.archives.gov/exhibits/charters/declaration_transcript.html.

We commonly refer to great athletes, actors, singers, and artists as "gifted" people, meaning they were born with special talents and abilities that enable them to do great things in their field. Excellence at anything requires hard work and discipline. But let's face it. Few of us have the athleticism of Michael Jordan, the singing voice of Frank Sinatra, or the technology genius of Bill Gates. We all tend to admire (and even covet) the gifts of "special" people.

But there *is* a very special gift that God has given *every* human being. You have it, your children have it, your next-door neighbor has it, and I have it. In many ways, it is the most amazing and powerful gift of all. The problem is that this gift is largely unrecognized, seriously underdeveloped, and almost universally underappreciated. I am speaking about the powerful gift of imagination.

Mouthwatering Power

If the thought of eating a particular food ever made your mouth water, you have experienced the power of imagination. Scientists tell us that our mouths water because the sight or thought of eating a particular food triggers our salivary glands, which is an essential function of our digestive system. Just an image inside of us, the image of eating food, has the power to make the body respond!

If you've ever been lost in a daydream, you've experienced the power of imagination. I remember the long, hot days of sitting in classrooms as a child, back in the days before air-conditioning. The teacher's voice would fade as I thought about going fishing with my dad or heading to Little League baseball practice after the final bell rang. These little "escapes" that took place in my mind would, for a few moments, at least, lift my soul above the humdrum world of Mr. Grissom's biology class.

If you've ever been in the midst of an unpleasant experience and consciously turned your mind to happier thoughts, you've used the power of imagination. My worst nightmare is visiting the dentist. I simply hate to recline on my back and "open wide" while someone I don't know inserts all kinds of sharp, pointy metal instruments into my mouth. To me, the worst sound in the world is the dentist's drill whirring and whining away as it vibrates my cranium. So how do I deal with a trip to the dentist? I replace what I can see with what I can't see. I use my imagination. My body may be under assault, but my mind is on the golf course. Hey, it helps. And if you've done the same thing in similar situations, you've used the power of imagination.

If you've ever been confronted with a problem that needs a quick fix, thought, *What can patch this?* and then headed inside for the duct tape, you've used the power of imagination.

If you've ever lifted your mood by looking forward to an event, you've used the power of imagination. We all love a good vacation. And for me, one of the greatest things about a two-week vacation is the three months prior to the getaway, when I am mentally *anticipating* that season of rest. In the midst of the daily grind, I can close my eyes and see myself on the beach. And it helps. If you've ever done anything like that, then you've used the power of imagination.

Imagination is God's gift to you. You already know how to use it, and you already *are* using it daily, but perhaps you haven't realized the fullness of its potential. Maybe you don't yet know that your imagination makes all things possible.

The Gift That Makes All Things Possible

The fuse for the dynamite in this book was ignited many years ago during a simple devotional reading of the construction of Babylon in Genesis 11. In a flash of revelation, the Lord showed me that imagination is the gift He has given to us that makes all things possible.

> *And the Lord said, Behold, they are one people and they have all one language; and this is only the beginning of what they will do, and now nothing they have imagined they can do will be impossible for them.* (Genesis 11:6 AMP)

Notice that, in the midst of man's undertaking to build Babylon, God makes an astounding statement: "**Nothing** they have **imagined** they can do **will be impossible** for them."

This is not the opinion of some business guru or New Age philosopher. This is God. *Nothing man imagines will be impossible for him.* It has always struck me as ironic that the Lord gave me this powerful revelation in an obviously negative context. These men were building something contrary to the will of God. Throughout Scripture, Babylon is a metaphor for all that displeases God. These wicked men had set about the building of what Saint Augustine called the "city of man."[8] In their prideful ambition, they imagined that they could make a name for themselves by constructing a "utopian" society and political system... *without God.*

The idea of building the city of Babylon was an "evil imagination." (We will talk more about "evil imaginations" in chapter 5.) God was not pleased with what they were doing, and He literally came down from heaven to stop their construction. But the story raises an interesting question: If human imagination can be such a powerful force for evil, how much more powerful can it be for good? What if we who love God and His kingdom learned to be

---

8. Saint Augustine of Hippo, *The City of God* (Peabody, MA: Hendrickson Publishers, 2009).

in unity, speak the same things, and use the power of imagination to build the city of God and advance His kingdom?

God Himself says that there is enough power in our human imagination to make all things possible. Anything *that* powerful needs to be recognized, celebrated, and cultivated within us. So let's take a closer look at the imagination.

Imagination: What Is It?

Words are fascinating to me. It never ceases to amaze me how looking up a word in the dictionary enriches and expands my understanding and appreciation of a term, even if it's a word that I commonly use. The definition of imagination is particularly enlightening.

Imagination: the act or power of forming a mental image of something not present to the senses or never before wholly perceived in reality; creative ability; a creation of the mind.[9]

Let us carefully unpack this definition:

+ Notice that imagination is an "act"; it's something we can do.

+ Imagination is a "power"; as human beings, we have within us the power to form "a mental image" of something not yet present to the physical senses.

---

9. "Imagination," Merriam-Webster Online, http://www.merriam-webster.com/dictionary/imagination (accessed August 8, 2015).

+ Imagination is "creative ability"; it's something that *precedes* the actual creation (more on this in chapter 2).

+ Imagination is, first and foremost, "a creation of the mind"; we use our imagination at the metaphysical level; physical activity is not involved.

Imagination Comes First

Imagination is the *primary* activity in any creative process.

Before the Babylonians set about building the city, they had *imagined* the city. Imagination (ideas, dreams) always comes first; everything we can see with our physical eyes began with an imagination or an idea in the mind. The Babylonians could have never built something they had not first imagined. So, imagination is what we might call a "first creation." They built Babylon, but the principle they used applies to every building ever constructed.

The first time Elizabeth and I went to Los Angeles, we had a list of things we wanted to see and do. At the top of our list was visiting Robert Schuller's Crystal Cathedral in Garden Grove, California. We had watched *Hour of Power* many times on TV, and I had read his book, which described how the first services at the church were held in a drive-in theater but then how eventually, Schuller began to imagine a spectacular church facility made of glass. Nothing like this had ever been built before and the challenges of constructing such a project were staggering. Many architects told Schuller that it couldn't be done. Really, how could a person build anything that big out of glass? But Schuller had a dream, and it was built, to the tune of eighteen million dollars!

The architects drew on their considerable experience with crystalline shapes and glass-covered galleries, as well as with auditoriums. The idea is to get people as close to the performance as possible...Translated into primary geometries, it became a four-pointed star, with free-standing balconies in three points and the chancel in the fourth. The connection with reality is maintained through ten thousand panes of glass hung on a space-frame scaffolding like a gigantic transparent tent. From the outside its quartz-like facets shimmer in one another's mirrored surfaces and reflective pond below. Inside, the mood is hushed, the filtered light lending a cool expectant atmosphere.[10]

The Crystal Cathedral, Garden Grove, California.

Schuller imagined it; architect Phillip Johnson designed it; and, four years later, in 1980, it was completed. If you've ever been there, you know what an amazing building it is. Sadly, the church filed for bankruptcy in 2010 and has moved on to less spectacular facilities. But the point is made. *Imagination comes first.*

10. Nory Miller, *Architecture: The Buildings and Projects of Philip Johnson and John Burgee* (New York: Random House, 1979), 111.

A common term in many of Robert Schuller's messages was "possibility thinking." And while I don't agree with all his theology, I can certainly admire his creative imagination; Schuller was a creative dreamer. But we all need to realize that the gift of imagination is not parceled out to just a few; we all have it!

Doing What Comes Naturally

The truth is that using our imagination comes naturally to us. It is so instinctive that we actually do it without thinking about it.

Let's say you are thinking about taking up golf. You have friends who play and want you to join them. So you begin a decision process, reasoning out the pros (it provides fellowship with friends, exercise, and is a sport you can play up into your senior years) and the cons (it costs money, it takes time, and it can be frustrating). Rationalizing the pros and cons is fine. But, at the end of the day, the determining factor will be whether or not you can *see* yourself getting into golf! Ultimately, your decision will be made in your imagination. If you can imagine yourself getting into golf, you'll discover an enabling power to purchase the equipment, take the lessons, and book the tee time! You may play golf for the rest of your life, but you would have never gotten into it unless you had first imagined yourself doing it. Doing any new thing always begins in the unseen, inner world of our imaginations.

When I say that the "seen" originates in the "unseen," some of you may think that I am advocating an unbiblical concept or metaphysical New Age philosophy. There is no question that New Agers and pop psychologists promote this same concept (read more on this in chapter 5), but I believe that they have "hijacked" biblical truth. Many have made millions using their imaginations while leaving the Bible and God out of the equa-tion. Non-believers routinely hack into God's programming and steal what belongs to us. Like the Babylonians, they pervert the principles in God's Word to build their empires and refuse to acknowledge Him or give Him the glory. But this doesn't change the fact that the Bible consistently teaches us that what is seen always originates in the realm of the unseen.

Indeed, this is exactly how God made the world! The Word of God confirms that the world came out of something we cannot see—the imagination of God:

Through faith we understand that the worlds were framed by the word of God, so that things which are seen were not made of things which do appear. (Hebrews 11:3 KJV)

Stop. Read that again. And again. This is one of the most profound revelations in all of Scripture. Don't just glance over this verse, because wrapping your arms around this great truth will become the foundation for releasing the power of imagina-tion in your own world.

Hebrews 11:3 teaches us that everything we can see is made out of something we cannot see. This means that everything we can see preexisted in the mind of the God. Everything we see had a preexistent condition.

God imagined what He wanted to create, then spoke it into existence! (See, for example, Genesis 1:3.) There was an image inside the mind and will of God that *preceded* everything He made. A Russian religious and political philosopher Nikolai Berdyaev perfectly captured this thought when he said, "God created the world through imagination."

If imagination is the power that created the universe, and God has given this power to us, then it must be one of God's greatest gifts! In all of creation, the power to form a mental image of something yet unseen is unique to human beings, who were created in the very image and likeness of God. (See Genesis 1:27.) Fish don't have it. Birds don't have it. Animals don't have it. Granted, there are some smart animals. We have a Maltese dog named Max who is very smart, but I'm pretty sure he doesn't sit around and dream about a better future! No, God exclusively reserved this amazing gift for *us*. The question then becomes, how do we use it?

We Live Our Lives "Inside Out"

You and I have the power to dream, desire, envision, and imagine. We have the ability to form "inner images" in our minds. So let us examine how these inner images are powerful life forces that determine how we live.

The inner images we have in our minds about ourselves (our identity) and the world around us (our worldview) always set the course for how we live and make decisions. We truly do live our lives "inside out."

It might shock you to realize that, right now, you are living your life according to the most dominant images inside you. The circumstances that you see around you have been created by the images within yourself. The world around you has been created from the world within yourself.

So how is that working for you? Not so great? Could be better? Would you like to see a change? Okay! You can get a fresh start in life by realizing that changing what you see on the inside actually has the power to create what you will see on the outside!

You may feel dominated by your circumstances and environment, by the things you can see. You may be working hard to change all these things for the better. But that approach achieves limited results, because the fundamental problem is never *outside* of us, it is always *inside* of us!

The same power that makes your mouth water can affect greater things in your life. The right place to start is always on the inside, learning to use the power God has given us to dream, to envision, and to imagine.

Always remember that the seen world came out of an unseen world, the imagination of God. So the seen world is actually the second creation. It exists in the visible world only because it *first* existed in the mind of the Maker. This is a revelation that can literally transform your life—*everything is created twice!*

2

UNDERSTANDING THE FIRST AND SECOND CREATIONS

I t bugs me that worldly people are sometimes smarter than God's people. In Jesus' parable of the unjust steward, the lord pays his wayward employee a backhanded compliment:

> *And the lord commended the unjust steward, because he had done wisely: for the children of this world are in their genera-tion wiser than the children of light.* (Luke 16:8 KJV)

Ouch! It ought to bother us that worldly people seem to run way ahead of God's people when it comes to understanding the power of imagination. In researching for this book, I couldn't help but notice that some of the most profound comments and quotes on the subject of imagination have come from people *outside* the church.

Napoleon Bonaparte (1769–1821) rose to power during the latter stages of the French Revolution, conquered most of Europe, and proclaimed himself as emperor. He was a soldier, and his battlefield strategies are still studied in military academies today. There seems to be no evidence that he was a Christian, but he must have given a lot of thought to the power of imagination to say something like this:

"Imagination rules the world."
—*Napoleon Bonaparte*

Albert Einstein (1879–1955) was a scientific genius whose simple formula $E=mc^2$ unlocked the secret of atomic power. But he was also an atheist—or, at least, an agnostic. Though he may have denied the existence of God, he did understand the power of imagination! As he said, "the true sign of intelligence is not knowledge but imagination." In Einstein's value system,

"Imagination is more important than knowledge."
—*Albert Einstein*

Carl Sagan (1934–1996) was an enormously gifted astronomer, astrophysicist, and educator. Millions have watched his TV series *Cosmos: A Personal Voyage*. Sagan was an agnostic; he did not believe in a personal God or in the biblical account of creation. Sagan did not know God, but he did know something about the power of imagination:

"Imagination will often carry us to worlds that never were, but without it we go nowhere."
—*Carl Sagan*

Muhammad Ali, one of the greatest prizefighters of all time, is Muslim, and he too has given some thought to the power of imagination:

"The man who has no imagination has no wings."
—*Muhammad Ali*

Why do the children of this world seem to know more about the power of imagination than the children of God?

Up until now, if you wanted to explore the power of imagination, you had to look outside the church. I've been studying this subject for over twenty years, and I'm sad to say that much of what I've learned about it did not come from within the church but from business books and the biographies of the rich and famous. The children of this world get it. They understand that the power of imagination is where all the great success stories begin.

Brian Tracy is an author and professional development trainer who has done a lot of research on the common denominator shared by successful people. Here's what he found:

> All successful people, men and women, are big dreamers. They imagine what their future could be, ideal in every respect, and then they work every day toward their distant vision, that goal or purpose.[11]

One of the greatest revelations about the power of imagination came to me twenty years ago as I was reading a business book written by a Mormon! Stephen Covey's best seller, *The 7 Habits of Highly Effective People*, is, in my opinion, one of the greatest business books of all time. After researching the lives and careers of hundreds of highly successful people, Covey identified seven habits they all shared in common. I could recommend that you adopt all of these healthy habits, but the second habit particularly applies to the subject of this book. Covey discovered that all highly successful people begin with the end in mind. Their starting place is in the *mind*. He goes on to show how beginning with the end in mind works because "all things are created twice."[12]

Four Words That Can Change Your Life

Everything is created twice. The revelation contained in these four words can change your life. People who get to the top use their imagination to envision their destination at the start of every endeavor. They know where they are going before they begin. They dream it before they do it. Successful people begin

---

11. Brian Tracy, *Create Your Own Future: How to Master the 12 Critical Factors of Unlimited Success* (Hoboken, NJ: John Wiley & Sons, Inc., 2002).
12. Stephen R. Covey, *The 7 Habits of Highly Effective People* (New York, NY: Simon & Schuster, 1989), 99.

with the end in mind because they know that *everything is created twice.*

The fact that everything is created twice means that there are always *two* creations: there is a mental image of a desired result, or a "first creation," that precedes the "second creation," which takes place in the physical realm.

Look at it this way. The first creation occurs in the spiritual realm, while the second creation takes place in the physical realm. The first creation refers to that which you cannot see with your physical eyes, because it takes place in the imagination. It is a vision, original idea, or dream within your own mind or the deepest desires of your heart. The second creation refers to everything you can see with your physical eyes.

You must begin with the end in mind. If you want to change the world *around* you, you must first change the world *within* you. This is a law!

The first creation must precede the second creation in order for a new creation to take place. If we cannot first see something in our mind or spirit (as in the first creation), we will never see it on the outside, in the physical, visible world (as in the second creation). We have to dream it before we will do it.

The Two Realms of Reality

Let us be clear on this. First and second creations are both realities. We live in a physical world, so it may seem that physical things are more real than spiritual things, but the Bible assures us that this is not so. The world we see is real. But the world we see came out of God and from God, whom we cannot see. As we shall see in a moment, the world existed first in the imagination of God before it became incarnated reality. God Himself began with the end in mind. In the same way God created the world,

His vision becoming a reality, so our imaginations, dreams, and desires are the spiritual substance of the things we are hoping for, the things we desire to see come to pass in the visible world.

In this book, we are focusing on the power of first creations, which take place outside of the physical realm. They are the imaginations, dreams, and visions that precede the second creations in the world around us. We might sum it up this way:

+ We must always begin with the end in mind because everything is created twice.

+ First creations are *spiritual* realities; second creations are *physical* realities.

+ All second creations are *physical* realities that originate as first creations in the realm of *spiritual* reality.

Take a few moments to apply this revelation right now in three simple steps:

1. **Observe.** Take a moment and look around you. What do you see? Perhaps...

+ This book you are reading.

+ The house you are living in.

+ The room you are sitting in.

+ The furniture you are sitting on.

+ The lamp that's casting light in the room.

2. **Recognize.** Acknowledge the fact that if you can see it, it's a second creation!

3. **Realize.** Celebrate the realization that everything you see had a first creation in the mind or imagination of the one who invented or designed it. Give yourself some time to embrace the revelation that everything you can see had its origin in what you cannot see.

If you can see it, it's a second creation. It had a previous existence as a first creation in the mind of the one who designed it. Whether it's something as simple as a pencil or as complex as a desktop computer, it wouldn't be visible to the physical eye unless it preexisted in a vision, dream, or imagination.

For example, I have worn contact lenses for almost fifty years. Eyeglasses and spectacles have been around for centuries. But somewhere, sometime, somebody had an idea. Somebody imagined that the glass lenses in an eyeglass frame could be effectively replaced by lenses that rest on the eyeball. If that person had not imagined it, I wouldn't be wearing contact lenses as I write this!

Every day, most of us use a cell phone, watch TV, or listen to the radio. We take all these modern-day "miracles" for granted. But they didn't just happen. Where did they begin? Where did they originate? The cell phone you talk through, the TV you watch, and the radio you listen to all began in someone's imagination.

- Alexander Graham Bell imagined the possibility of people talking to each other over vast distances before he invented the telephone. He succeeded. But the telephone he imagined and built required wires. A hundred years later, a new generation would dream of telephones without wires. So now we all have cell phones that work on wireless networks!

- Someone imagined that sound could be broadcast through the air, and radio was invented. A generation later, someone imagined that images as well as sound could be broadcast through the air, and television was invented.

- This book you are reading is a second creation. You can see it before you only because I saw it in my spirit as a first creation many years ago.

Everything is created twice. Everything begins with a dream—an imagination or inner image of what could be done. The dreams, desires, and ideas that spring forth in our imaginations are all first creations that take place in the unseen realm. Every advancement in mankind's quality of life found its origin in the mind of someone who knew how to use the power of their God-given imagination.

Having even an elementary understanding of the first and second creations allows us to draw some very powerful conclusions:

+ The invisible realm is more powerful than the visible realm because that which is seen owes its very existence to that which is unseen.

+ What is inside of us is more powerful than what is outside of us, because what is outside of us is created by what is inside of us.

+ If we want to change the world *around* us, we must change the world *within* us. Our starting point is the unseen realm of our ideas, dreams, desires, and imagination.

God Created the World by Imagination

We can know that everything is created twice, not because a great business book written by a Mormon says so and not because I say so, but because the Bible clearly demonstrates and explains it.

Let's revisit Hebrews 11:3 (KJV).

Through faith we understand that the worlds were framed by the word of God, so that things which are seen were not made of things which do appear.

My faith in God's Word allows me to understand that everything is created twice. The things which I see are actually second creations. They originated as first creations. The things I see are made out of things I cannot see.

Let me paraphrase this amazing Scripture in light of what we've learned so far: Things that are seen (second creations) were not made of things that do appear to our physical eye, but were instead made by the word of God (invisible first creation).

This means that the earth and everything in it, including you and I, is a second creation, the incarnation of a first creation that took place in the mind of God and was breathed out in His words. Or, to repeat one brilliant writer, "God created the world by imagination" (Nikolai Berdyaev).

The human race is unique in all creation because God made man and woman in His own image and likeness. We are not God! But we are God-like in our ability to create. This explains why, throughout history, mankind is constantly building, creating, and inventing things.

Dorothy Sayers was an amazing author and a friend of C. S. Lewis. In her classic book, *The Mind of the Maker*, she comments on how man carries the stamp of His Creator in his compulsion to create: "The characteristic common to God and man is apparently...the desire and the ability to make things."[13]

Nothing confirms our creation more than this: the power we have within us to imagine, to dream, and to make things. Again, Berdyaev states the case for creativity so well.

God created man in his own image and likeness, i.e., made him a creator too, calling him to free spontaneous

---

13. Dorothy Sayers, *The Mind of the Maker* (London: Bloomsbury Publishing, 1941, 1994), 17.

activity…. Free creativeness is the creature's answer to the great call of its creator. Man's creative work is the fulfill-ment of the Creator's secret will.[14]

When we create things, we fulfill God's will for our lives. We make a big mistake when we see only the creativity in others. We are creative, too! Your creativity may be dormant because you haven't been operating in the power of imagination. But God is the Father of the entire human race, and He delights in our ability to act like Him in spontaneous creativity. Without this remarkable power of imagination, the quality of life we enjoy today would have never been possible.

Think of all the great inventions and advancements throughout human history, and realize that all of them follow this unbreakable law: Everything is created twice. If something exists, someone had to think of it. Someone had to have a cre-ative idea. Dr. Raymond Holliwell puts it this way: "An idea is an image or a picture in the mind. There must have been an idea, a mental picture, back of every well-known achievement and invention."[15]

"I've Got a Great Idea"

God has programmed us to think in images and pictures. If you've ever said "I've got a great idea," you have operated in the power of God-given imagination. We live in a world made pos-sible by those who have had great ideas.

+ If you own a piece of wool clothing, it exists because some-one, somewhere, had the idea of shearing a sheep and making a garment out of it.

14. Nikolai Berdyaev, *The Destiny of Man.*
15. Raymond Holliwell, *Working with the Law* (Camarillo, CA: DeVorss & Company, 2005), 6.

+ If you have a drinking glass in your cabinet, it exists because someone had an idea that sand could be converted into glass.

+ The words you are reading at this very moment are printed on a piece of paper because someone figured out a more efficient way to use wood pulp.

When God created Adam, He gave him dominion over the earth. There is no more "earth" present today than there was when Adam was in the garden. So where did all the buildings, streets, cell phones, and automobiles come from? Out of the earth! All the wondrous inventions and constructions in our world today came out of the original raw material God gave to man in the creation. All our modern conveniences and achievements are a testimony to the creative power of man made in the image and likeness of God!

I am certainly not the first to write about this God-given (and God-like) gift that motivates us to dream, envision, and imagine things not yet seen. Every creative work of art, including paintings, books, and musical compositions, is really a manifestation of the Creator's inner imagination, where it first existed.

The world of the creative arts

I have hundreds of books in my personal library. Every one of them is a second creation. Their first creation took place in the heart, mind, and imagination of their authors. As one author said, wittily demonstrating this point, "My book is finished—I have only to write it."[16]

History tells us that the classical music of Wolfgang Amadeus Mozart was composed in his head before he ever wrote it down in musical notations. Ludwig van Beethoven's greatest works were written after he became totally deaf. Biographers tell

16. Dorothy Sayers, *The Mind of the Maker*, 81.

us that he "heard" music in his head and wrote from there. So when we listen to Beethoven's String Quartet No. 14 in C-Sharp Minor, we really listen to a second creation! Every song ever written takes place in the composer's mind before it ever finds its way onto paper.

An interviewer once asked the great sculptor Michelangelo how he created one of his amazing sculptural works. He replied, "I saw the angel in the marble and carved until I set him free." A thousand men can look at a block of marble, but only someone using his God-given imagination can see an angel inside it.

Or again, I really love movies, and since a movie is something I can see, I know that it is a second creation. I'm looking at the finished product of somebody's fertile imagination. In all the history of American film writers, no one had a more powerful imagination than Walt Disney. At the posthumous dedication of one of Walt Disney's parks, someone commented to Walt's surviving brother Roy Disney, "I wish Walt would have been alive to see this." Roy replied, "Walt *did* see it. If he hadn't seen it, we wouldn't be seeing it."

Walt Disney was a dreamer. As I mentioned earlier, he called his creative team "The Imagineers." I remember growing up watching *The Wonderful World of Disney*, one of the first network television series in color. The theme song of the show was "When You Wish upon a Star," from the classic cartoon film *Pinocchio*. Every kid knows how the song says that when your heart is in a dream and you wish it upon a star, your dream will come true! It's certainly a secular song—I am not encouraging you to wish upon a star, unless it's Jesus, the *"bright and morning star"* of Revelation 22:16! But the song *is* a great illustration of the first and second creations. The songwriter probably never knew how close he'd come to biblical revelation!

Partnering with God

When you begin to use your God-given imagination, you are actually coming into alignment and partnership with God's order of creation, where all things are possible. And now you know where to start. You begin with the end in mind. You now know that everything is created twice, and that if you want to change the world *around* you, you must begin by changing world *within* you, using your God-given imagination.

When you do, you'll discover an amazing ancillary benefit. You will find that there is power in your hopes and dreams that will uplift you and keep you strong through the winds and the storms of life. There is sustaining power in a God-given dream!

3

THE SUSTAINING POWER OF IMAGINATION

I would have lost heart, unless I had believed that I would
see the goodness of the LORD in the land of the living.
—Psalm 27:13 (NKJV)

This book is about releasing the power of imagination within us to change the world around us. It presupposes that the world around us needs to be changed—and that is no secret! While we live in the greatest nation on earth, who would deny the abundant evidence around us that our nation is declining and that our culture is deteriorating right before our very eyes? We are trillions of dollars in debt. We continue to murder the unborn with a death count of fifty-three million and rising. Our religious freedoms are being threatened by the IRS and an overreaching federal government. The institution of marriage has been redefined, and traditional family values are under attack. Meanwhile, a virtual mudslide of moral erosion is engulfing many families and sweeping them into an abyss of value abdication.

It's easy to lose heart if we forget that we will see the goodness of the Lord in our lifetime. (See Psalm 27:13.) We all know that we need our faith in hard times. But we also need to realize how God uses the power of imagination and dreams to sustain us until the breakthroughs come.

Life Is Difficult; Deal with It!

This book was not written as some kind of self-help manual for creating your own metaphysical dreamworld. I am not encouraging you to fantasize your way out of a problem or to rely on simplistic positive thinking, which is really nothing more than denial. On the contrary, I begin with the presupposition that life is difficult because we are living in a sinful world. This is an important place to begin, because it is the truth.

"Life is difficult. This is a great truth, one of the greatest truths."[17] Some of you may recognize this statement as the premise of Dr. Scott Peck's best-selling book *The Road Less Traveled*. This book has sold over seven million copies and was on the New York Times best seller list for ten years! The book challenges the reader to embrace the sobering truth that life is difficult, claiming that embracing it will help the reader to deal with life much better. In effect, he invites us to take off our rose-colored glasses and recognize that the frustrations, complications, and difficulties we experience in life are normal and common to all men.

Peck's premise is true. Life is difficult. This is tough truth, indeed. And you might be one of those people who recoil in

---

17. Dr. M. Scott Peck, *The Road Less Traveled* (New York, NY: Simon & Schuster, 1978, 1985, 2002), 15.

response to it; accepting it continues to be a road less traveled in our nation today. We Americans don't like to hear truths that sound like negatives. We don't want to watch the news or deal with the staggering accumulation of our national debt. We don't want to get on the scales. We don't want to look at our bank balance. Human nature shies away from truth that seems negative. But truth is truth, and living in denial won't help us.

The apostle Paul had to correct the churches of Galatia because they had strayed away from sound doctrine. He confronted them with the unpopular truth and then asked, *"Have I now become your enemy because I am telling you the truth?"* (Galatians 4:16 NLT). Not much has changed since apostle Paul's day. If we don't like the news a messenger brings, we want to shoot him. Hearing the truth may be an unpleasant experience, but Jesus said that knowing the truth will set us free! (See John 8:32.) It just may be hard to handle.

"The truth will set you free, but first it makes you miserable."
—*Jamie Buckingham*

There is a considerable amount of pressure on Christian pastors today to focus on positive things, even at the expense of preaching the *"whole counsel of God"* (Acts 20:27 NKJV). It is no secret that many of our churches have abandoned teaching foundational theology on unhappy themes like the depravity of man and original sin. The tendency is to skip over the unpleasant stuff and focus on the subjects of love, mercy, and grace. I love to preach love, mercy, and grace messages, too, but I do not

understand how we can make strong disciples without equip-
ping the saints with God's explanation of why the world is so bad
and life is so difficult.

And life *is* difficult. Jesus said so! *"Remember the word that I
said unto you, The servant is not greater than his lord. If they have
persecuted me, they will also persecute you"* (John 15:20 KJV). And,
"In the world ye shall have tribulation" (John 16:33 KJV).

Paul said so! *"Indeed, all who desire to live godly in Christ Jesus
will be persecuted"* (2 Timothy 3:12).

Peter said so! *"Beloved, think it not strange concerning the fiery
trial which is to try you, as though some strange thing happened unto
you"* (1 Peter 4:12 KJV).

James said so! *"Consider it all joy, my brethren, when you
encounter various trials, knowing that the testing of your faith pro-
duces endurance"* (James 1:2–3).

Accepting the fact that life is difficult in a culture that wor-
ships comfort and convenience and seeks to avoid facing up to
harsh realities is helpful. I think Dr. Peck is right to encourage
us to accept that we live in a sinful world that is full of war, prejudice, and injustice, because that is reality.

Where Dr. Peck Goes Wrong

However, I believe he takes a wrong turn on the road less
traveled.

Okay, life is difficult. So far so good. But, in my opinion, Dr.
Peck goes too far when he argues that simply accepting life as
difficult removes its difficulty!

> [That life is difficult] is a great truth because once we truly
> see this truth, we transcend it. Once we truly know that

life is difficult—once we truly understand and accept it—then life is no longer difficult. Because once it is accepted, the fact that life is difficult no longer matters.[18]

I have never been able to agree with this conclusion. Dr. Peck maintains that once we simply accept that life is difficult, we transcend it, and life is no longer difficult—or, at least, the difficulties no longer matter. In other words, simply accepting life as difficult magically (my word, not his) catapults us over the difficulties of life. With all due respect to Dr. Peck, experiences in my own life, including ministering to others for over thirty years, have convinced me that we need a lot more than that. I don't believe that embracing the conviction "life is difficult" has any real power to sustain us through the actual difficulties of life.

God, however, has given us something that *will*.

We Need a Lively Hope

What we really need to sustain us through the difficulties of life are lively hopes, inspiring dreams, and faith for a preferred future. Life *is* difficult. We suffer disappointments and betrayals. We get tired. We feel like giving up. But simply knowing that life is difficult doesn't hold us up or inspire us. Instead, as I hope to show you in the Scriptures, the Lord uses hopes, dreams, and God-given imaginations to sustain us and keep us going through the difficulties of life.

Remember that your hopes and dreams are actually inner images of your preferred future. They are the first creations that contain the power to sustain and uphold you until the second creations come to pass. We need these because the greatest

18. Dr. M. Scott Peck, *The Road Less Traveled* (New York: Simon and Schuster, 2002), 15.

difficulties of life come in the waiting time between our dreams and their fulfillment. There is always a time gap between a promise and the fulfillment of that promise.

> "Between the promise and the provision, there's always a problem."
> —Kelley Varner

In Scripture, God promised Abraham a son, but Abraham still had to wait twenty-five years before Isaac was born. Later, God assured Abraham that his descendants would enter into the Promised Land, but several centuries passed before they took possession of it. God will give us desires, visions, and dreams. But there is always a delay between the promise and the provision.

You must not lose hope in the seasons of delay between the promise (the first creation) and the provision (the second creation). Hope is not a flimsy, whimsical wish; it is an anchor for our souls!

> *We…have fled for refuge in laying hold of the hope set before us. This hope we have as an anchor of the soul, both sure and steadfast.* (Hebrews 6:18–19 NKJV)

True, biblical hope comes to us in the form of inner images of the vision God has in mind for us. When those images are clear, alive, and strong, they have the power to sustain us through the delays and difficulties of life.

> *For in hope we have been saved, but hope that is seen is not hope; for who hopes for what he already sees? But if we hope*

*for what we do not see, with perseverance we wait eagerly for
it.* (Romans 8:24–25)

We don't need hope for what we can already see. We need
hope for *"what we do not see"* yet. Notice that it says that our
hope gives us the persistence to persevere until it is fulfilled.
Hope never works apart from faith. Hope and faith are not the
same thing, but they do work together.

*There are three things that remain—faith, hope, and love—
and the greatest of these is love.*
(1 Corinthians 13:13 TLB)

Faith is always in the present tense. Hope is always connected with the future and is the realm of the first creation. If
we don't hold on to hope, we will sink. *"Hope deferred makes the
heart sick"* (Proverbs 13:12). I can have faith and confidence that,
one day, I will go to heaven. But I need lively hope to sustain me
along the way!

Biblical Examples of Hope

Let's take a closer look at how God consistently used dreams
and imagination to strengthen the faith of His people in the delay
between the first and second creations, between the promise and
the provision, in the lives of Abraham, Isaac, Jacob, Joseph, and
the Lord Jesus Christ.

Abraham

Abraham is the prototype of faith for all who believe. God
promised Abraham a son when he was seventy-five years old. The
provision came with the birth of Isaac when he was one hundred
years old. The *problem* was the delay between the promise and
the provision. In spite of his great failure in the conception of

Ishmael, the Bible assures us that Abraham passed his test. Now notice what sustained him through the delay between the promise and provision:

> *Against all hope, Abraham in hope believed and so became*
> *the father of many nations, just as it had been said to him,*
> *"So shall your offspring be."*   (Romans 4:18 NIV)

This seems confusing—"*against all hope...in hope he believed.*" Against all human hope, which is limited to what he could see, Abraham in hope believed in the inner image given to him by God's promise, which he could not see, until his son was born. It was the God-given dream of being a father that bolstered his patience, anchored his soul, and preserved his emotions during the twenty-five years of delay.

Abraham is a "faith giant," and his journey is the model of our journey. He is called the "*father of all them that believe*" (Romans 4:11 KJV), and we are told to "*walk in the steps of that faith of our father Abraham*" (verse 12 KJV). He is the Old Testament prototype of the New Testament believer. We know that, in his case, there was a twenty-five-year delay between the promise and the provision.

Abraham was seventy-five years old and childless when God appeared to him, but God promised him that he would have a son and be the "*father of a multitude*" (Genesis 17:4). Notice the three images God used to sustain Abraham's faith during the difficulty of delay: an image of a new name, an image from the heavens, and an image from the earth.

1. *An image of a new name.* God changed Abram's name, which simply means "father," to Abraham, which means "*father of a multitude*" (Genesis 17:4). Names are important because they convey our identity. To the Hebrews, names communicated

"word pictures," or images. Abram longed for a child, but God wanted to see him not just as a father, but as the father of a multitude. The change of his name meant that every time he spoke his name or heard it spoken, the mental image *"father of a multitude"* was projected into his mind.

2. *An image from the heavens.* God took Abraham outside his tent and told him to consider the stars in the heavens, for they represented the number of descendants he would have!

> *And He took him outside and said, "Now look toward the heavens, and count the stars, if you are able to count them." And He said to him, "So shall your descendants be." Then he believed in the Lord.*　　　(Genesis 15:5–6)

God was using an *external* image to give Abraham an *internal* image. Notice the result of this exercise: *"Then he believed in the Lord."* God used the power of images to fuel his faith!

3. *An image from the earth.* Later, in addition to the image of the stars in the heavens, God gave Abraham a second powerful image:

> *Indeed I will greatly bless you, and I will greatly multiply your seed as the stars of the heavens and as the sand which is on the seashore; and your seed shall possess the gate of their enemies.*　　　(Genesis 22:17)

After using the image of the multitude of stars to build Abraham's faith, God added a second metaphor—the grains of sand on a seashore. Abraham had been to the beach. He had probably picked up a handful of sand and perhaps considered its construction—how many grains of sand were in one handful. (I discovered that there are people who have actually tried to figure this out; one source counted 40,000 grains of sand in one teaspoon!)

In both cases, God used *external* images, the stars and the sand, to build a strong *internal* image inside Abraham of the number of offspring he could expect. God was painting "images" inside of Abraham, the first creation that would later become fulfilled as second creation!

I have always believed that these images were prophetic in nature. God was revealing that Abraham would have a multitude born after the flesh, non-believing descendants, represented by the earthly sand, and also a multitude born after the Spirit, believing descendants, represented by the heavenly stars. And so it has turned out. There has truly been a multitude of non-believers who can trace their genealogy back to the earthly, natural seed of Abraham, represented by the sand. But, there has also been millions of believers, descendants in spirit and not in flesh, who can trace their salvation back to the heavenly seed of Abraham, represented by the stars. So the images of the sand and the stars are actually spiritual metaphors representing the earthly and heavenly descendants of this great man.

When Abraham foolishly attempted to bring about the promise of God by means of the flesh, Ishmael was born and became the father of the nations that have been at war with Israel and Christianity right up to this present day. Muslims call themselves the "sons of Ishmael," a fulfillment of what God showed Abraham in the sand. Later, Isaac was born as the son of the promise, a type of Christ, and the spiritual fulfillment of what God showed Abraham in the stars. We should not be surprised that modern Islam is at war with Israel and Christianity, because "*that which is born of the flesh is flesh; and that which is born of the Spirit is spirit*" (John 3:6 KJV). And again, "*The flesh sets its desire against the Spirit, and the Spirit against the flesh; for these are in opposition to one another"* (Galatians 5:17).

The flesh and the spirit can never peacefully coexist. The conflict in Abraham's household was between his promised son, Isaac, and his *"son of the bondwoman"* (KJV), Ishmael. Somebody had to go. *"Cast out the bondwoman and her son: for the son of the bondwoman shall not be heir with the son of the freewoman"* (Galatians 4:30 KJV).

All this imagery finds its roots in the garden of Eden. After Adam and Eve sinned, God pronounced judgment upon the serpent with a prophecy about two "seeds." *"And I will cause hostility between you and the woman, and between your offspring and her offspring"* (Genesis 3:15 NLT).

The Hebrew word for *offspring* means "seed," referencing posterity. The seed of the serpent is all who are born in the flesh. The seed of the woman represents all who are reborn in the Spirit.[19]

Abraham indeed became the father of many nations; he became the father of a heavenly seed, represented by the stars, and an earthly seed, represented by the sand. And even though Ishmael was a product of Abraham's lack of faith, God still promised to make a nation out of him: *"And also of the son of the bondwoman will I make a nation, because he is thy seed"* (Genesis 21:13 KJV).

It is doubtful how much of this Abraham understood, but it seems obvious that God used these inner images to sustain his faith between the promise and the provision. And if Abraham is the father (model, prototype) of all who believe, and we are

---

19. Bible scholars refer to Genesis 3:15 as the "proto-evangel," or the first mention of the coming of Christ in the Bible. Christ was the "seed of the woman" who came to "crush the serpent's head." (See Genesis 3:15.)

to "*walk in the steps of that faith of our father Abraham*" (Romans 4:12 KJV), might we not expect God to uphold our hope and faith in the same way, with God-given images?

Isaac

Later, God used the same approach to sustain the faith of Abraham's son Isaac.

> *And the* LORD *appeared to [Isaac] and said, "Do not go down to Egypt; stay in the land of which I shall tell you. Sojourn in this land and I will be with you and bless you, for to you and to your descendants I will give all these lands, and I will establish the oath which I swore to your father Abraham. I will multiply your descendants as the stars of heaven, and will give your descendants all these lands."*
> (Genesis 26:2–4)

Here we see God *renewing* the dream He gave Abraham with the next generation, again using images and metaphor as fuel for faith.

Jacob

The pattern continues with Isaac's son Jacob.

Jacob was the son of Isaac and the grandson of Abraham. He infamously stole the birthright of his elder brother, Esau, by deceiving his father. (See Genesis 27.) In spite of his methods, he received the blessing from his father. In Genesis 28, we find Jacob a fugitive, running away from home and the wrath of his brother. Surely he must have been at "low tide." So how did God sustain his faith and encourage him in the journey? *He gave him a dream!* The Lord visited Jacob in his sleep and showed him a ladder that connected heaven and earth.

> *He [Jacob] had a dream, and behold, a ladder was set on the earth with its top reaching to heaven; and behold, the angels of God were ascending and descending on it. And behold, the Lord stood above it and said, "I am the Lord, the God of your father Abraham and the God of Isaac; the land on which you lie, I will give it to you and to your descendants. Your descendants will also be like the dust of the earth, and you will spread out to the west and to the east and to the north and to the south; and in you and in your descendants shall all the families of the earth be blessed. Behold, I am with you and will keep you wherever you go, and will bring you back to this land; for I will not leave you until I have done what I have promised you."* (Genesis 28:12–15)

Jacob's ladder was actually a powerful image of the open heaven that would be fulfilled by the Messiah. (See Genesis 28:10–17.) But in the moment, God used that particular image to encourage Jacob and sustain his faith in the many long years of waiting that lay ahead of him.

By now, the pattern established in the lives of Abraham, Isaac, and Jacob is clear. God uses God-given imaginations, hopes, and dreams to sustain His people during the difficult days between the first and second creations.

But there's more.

Joseph

In the same way God used images and dreams for Abraham, Isaac, and Jacob, He used dreams to encourage Jacob's son Joseph. God visited Joseph as a young man by means of dreams. Dreams are internal images, which are powerful because they are image-based. Joseph dreamed in vivid images. Here's his first dream:

Then Joseph had a dream, and when he told it to his broth-
ers, they hated him even more. He said to them, "Please
listen to this dream which I have had; for behold, we were
binding sheaves in the field, and lo, my sheaf rose up and
also stood erect; and behold, your sheaves gathered around
and bowed down to my sheaf." Then his brothers said to
him, "Are you actually going to reign over us? Or are you
really going to rule over us?" So they hated him even more
for his dreams and for his words.   (Genesis 37:5–8)

In his dream, Joseph saw himself and his brothers gathering wheat. Then he saw all his brother's stacks bowing down to his stack. What a powerful pictorial image of promotion, exaltation, power, and authority. Joseph interpreted this to be God's picture of what his future would look like.

But God wasn't finished. He gave Joseph a second dream.

Now he had still another dream, and related it to his broth-
ers, and said, "Lo, I have had still another dream; and
behold, the sun and the moon and eleven stars were bowing
down to me." He related it to his father and to his brothers;
and his father rebuked him and said to him, "What is this
dream that you have had? Shall I and your mother and your
brothers actually come to bow ourselves down before you to
the ground?" His brothers were jealous of him, but his father
kept the saying in mind.   (Genesis 37:9–11)

Notice that in the two dreams, the images were different, but the principles of future promotion, exaltation, power, and authority were the same. We can learn several important principles about God-given imaginations from Joseph.

1. God is the Giver of powerful inner images (first creations) that He plans to bring to pass in our future (second creations).

God-given imaginations communicate God's plan for our lives. *"For I know the plans that I have for you,' declares the LORD, 'plans for welfare and not for calamity to give you a future and a hope'"* (Jeremiah 29:11).

2. Telling God's plan to a "half brother" might get you into trouble.

Joseph was a son of Jacob, but he had a different mother from his brothers. Sharing your dreams with a half brother may not be a good idea. We should be careful about sharing our God-given imaginations with those whose hearts aren't right with God. We need to understand that God-given dreams can elicit hatred (see Genesis 37:8) and envy (see Genesis 37:11) in those who don't have their own dream from God. Even our parents may rebuke us. (See Genesis 37:10.) In other words, your dreams can get you into trouble if you don't steward them wisely and use discretion in who you tell them to.

3. The third lesson we learn from Joseph confirms the theme of this chapter: God-given imaginations (dreams) have the power to sustain us through the difficult delays between the first and second creations.

God knew Joseph's future would contain promotion and exaltation, but He also knew what Joseph would have to go through to get there. I am personally persuaded that it is our God-given dreams that sustain and strengthen us as we endure Joseph-like trials and delays, such as…

+ Betrayals. Joseph's brothers sold him out. (See Genesis 37:18–28.) Have you ever been betrayed?

+ False accusations. Potiphar's wife lied about Joseph, accusing him of trying to seduce her, which got him thrown into prison. (See Genesis 39:7–22.) Have you ever been falsely accused?

✦ Unjust punishments. Bible scholars calculate that Joseph languished in an Egyptian prison for about thirteen years before his deliverance—all for something he didn't do. Have you ever suffered for something you didn't do?

Yet, with all these problems, there is no indication that Joseph's faith ever failed. Joseph's faith in the first creation (his dreams) sustained him until they were fulfilled in the second creation. The psalmist would later give us more insight into God's purpose behind Joseph's trials.

> *Joseph…was sold as a slave. They afflicted his feet with fetters, he himself was laid in irons; until the time that his word came to pass, the word of the Lord tested him.*
> (Psalm 105:17–19)

I like how the *New Living Translation* puts this:

> *They bruised his feet with fetters and placed his neck in an iron collar. Until the time came to fulfill his dreams, the Lord tested Joseph's character. Then Pharaoh sent for him and set him free; the ruler of the nation opened his prison door.*   (Psalm 105:18–20 NLT)

God never wastes a hurt. He is always at work, even when we are tried and tested as we wait for the fulfillment of our dreams. There is always a delay between the first and second creations. Those delays can include many forms of suffering, as it was in Joseph's case. Life is difficult, but the lesson here is that Joseph's faith didn't fail because God-given imaginations, visions, and dreams fueled his faith in the long delays on the road to his destiny.

The same holds true for us. God-given dreams and imaginations contain incredible power to sustain us in faith through the trials and tribulations that arise on our journey toward their fulfillment.

"If the dream is big enough, the facts don't matter."
—Dr. Mark Chironna

Temptations to sin, trials, and troubles may come, but God-given dreams (or imaginations) have the power to get us through. The images inside Abraham and the dreams inside Joseph sustained them as they waited on the promise of the Father.

Jesus

However, the ultimate illustration of this truth is found in none other than the Lord Jesus Christ Himself.

We can look to Abraham and Joseph as models of the sustaining power of God-given imaginations; but in Hebrews 12, we are told to "[look] *unto Jesus*" who is the "*author* [of the first creation] *and finisher* [of the second creation] *of our faith*" (Hebrews 12:2 KJV).

Jesus had the promise of the Father, the redemption of all who would believe, as a first creation. The provision would come as a second-creation reality. Between the promise and the provision, however, was a huge problem—the cross!

How did God sustain His only Son in His hour of trial? Oh, dear reader, don't miss this! "[Jesus] *who for the joy that was set before him endured the cross, despising the shame, and is set down at the right hand of the throne of God*" (Hebrews 12:2 KJV).

Here we are told that it was the *"joy that was set before him"* that sustained Jesus through the terrible ordeal of the cross. So what was the *"joy that was set before him"*? I believe it was the "inner image" of what His suffering would procure—the redemption of you and me! Even as He hung on the tree, Jesus beheld (inside Himself) the image of the redeemed community He was dying for!

Isaiah 53 is one of the most famous messianic prophecies concerning the sufferings of Christ on the cross, and it confirms our theme.

> *When You make His soul an offering for sin, He shall see His seed, He shall prolong His days, and the pleasure of the Lord shall prosper in His hand. He shall see the labor of His soul, and be satisfied. By His knowledge My righteous Servant shall justify many, for He shall bear their iniquities.* (Isaiah 53:10–11 NKJV)

In this prophetic vision, Isaiah saw that the Messiah, in the midst of His suffering, would *"see His seed"* (verse 11) and *"the labor of His soul, and be satisfied"* (verse 12). How can we miss this? Jesus endured the cross by "seeing" the inner image of you, me, and all the redeemed who would be the result of His labor, and it *"satisfied"* Him!

Too many believers fail in their faith because there's no strong dream or inner image to get them through their trouble. Just before Hebrews 12:2 tells us that Jesus endured the cross for the joy that was set before Him, Hebrews 12:1 tells us to *"lay aside every weight, and the sin which doth so easily beset us, and... run with patience the race that is set before us"* (KJV). So how do we do it? Hebrews 12:3 says that we do it by *"looking unto Jesus"* as our model. We do it the same way He did it—by having an "inner image" of the joy we will have when we see the second creation.

Do You Have a Dream to Sustain You?

Life is difficult. You will suffer disappointments, betrayals, and delays. If Abraham, Isaac, Jacob, Joseph, and Jesus needed the sustaining power of God-given hopes, dreams, and imaginations, you will, too.

If you don't have a dream or a clear imagination about your preferred future, get one. You may ask, "How do I do it?" The answer is so simple, it may surprise you.

4

PRAYERS THAT CREATE
THE FUTURE

It's tough to make predictions, especially about the future.
—Yogi Berra[20]

In our nation today, there is a lot of fear about the future, even among the ranks of Bible-believing Christians. There seems to be a prevailing sense of helplessness, a feeling that the future is something that is just going to "happen" to us, and after it does, we must just deal with it the best we can. I find that when I ask people to give me one word about how they see the future for themselves, their family, or our nation, I often hear these responses:

---

20. Yogi Berra was a catcher for the New York Yankees. He was elected to the National Baseball Hall of Fame in 1972 and is known for his witticisms, called "Yogiisms," such as "It ain't over till it's over," "Baseball is 90% mental, the other half is physical," and "You can observe a lot by watching."

- "Uncertain"
- "Scary"
- "Unpredictable"
- "Dangerous"

The truth is that there certainly are things coming our way that are outside of our control. But we have not been left to the mercy of fate or the actions of others. I want to show you how, in a very real sense, God has given us the power to create our future.

The idea of creating our future is not original to this book. The sixteenth president of the United States, "Honest Abe," said it this way: "The best way to predict your future is to create it."[21] Abraham Lincoln was undoubtedly one of America's greatest presidents. From his letters, journals, and speeches, we know that he believed in God and was a man of prayer. I am personally convinced that he understood the theory of the first and second creations, even if he did not use those terms. Consider again the opening lines of the Gettysburg Address, one of the most famous speeches in American history:

> Four score and seven years ago our fathers *brought forth*, upon this continent, a new nation, *conceived* in liberty, and dedicated to the proposition that "all men are created equal."[22]

---

21. Attributed to Abraham Lincoln. Some deny this to be an actual quote from Lincoln, attributing it to a much earlier source, the French playwright Molière, the pen name of Jean-Baptiste Poquelin (1622–1673). But even if Lincoln didn't say it, modern versions of the quote are found in the speeches and writings of some of today's top business consultant experts like Peter F. Drucker, Tom Peters, and Alan Kay. I believe this quote is an insightful paraphrase of what Jesus taught about prayer in Mark 11:22–24.
22. Lincoln, "Gettysburg Address", emphasis added.

Lincoln's speech confirms the powerful principle that everything is created twice. Notice the language here. He said that our forefathers "brought forth" what they had "conceived in liberty."

What they "brought forth" was the second creation, the result of what they had "conceived," the first creation. Our founding fathers were not content to let the future just happen to them. They prayed, imagined a new nation, and brought forth what they'd imagined. *They created the future.*

Is It Possible to Create Your Future?

Over the past few years, the idea of creating the future has been reintroduced to the American marketplace by some of the most creative and innovative minds of our times.

"The very best way to predict the future is to create it."
—Peter Drucker, *management consultant & author*

"The best way to predict the future is to invent it."
—Alan Kay, *computer expert*

Create the future. *Invent* the future. Whenever I see how powerful statements like these are having positive effects, such as energizing creativity in the marketplace, I automatically default to finding where these principles are expressed in the Word of God. As I've said before, all truth is God's truth but, sometimes, the world seems to outstrip the church in its application of the truth. Entrepreneurs and visionaries of our day obviously believe that we can create the future, and they are making millions doing it. I wrote this book to show God's people how we can create a kingdom future using the power of our God-given imagination.

The above quotes presuppose that we are not victims of our circumstances and that we can proactively shape our futures. What does it mean to be proactive?

Proactive: tending to initiate change rather than reacting to events...denoting a mental process that affects a subsequent process.[23]

If you are going to create the future, you must consciously and wholeheartedly take responsibility for your quality of life in the future. You must no longer see yourself as a victim of your circumstances or of the things that have happened to you. You must initiate change rather than simply react to events. You must believe that you can predict your future by creating it. It all begins in your *mind*.

If you are a Christian, you might dismiss these statements as sounding like New Age philosophy or Eastern mysticism, but I assure you that this is not the case. Indeed, I intend to prove

23. "Proactive," *Collins English Dictionary—Complete and Unabridged* (HarperCollins Publishers, 1991, 1994, 1998, 2000, 2003), http://www.thefreedictionary.com/proactive (accessed July 14, 2015).

to you that these quotes are actually just updated paraphrases of what Jesus taught us about the prayer of faith! (See Mark 11:22–24.)

The truth is that *you already know how to do this.*

Prayers That Create the Future

Let me ask you two questions: (1) Have you ever prayed? (2) Have your prayers ever been answered?

Almost every Christian would answer yes to these two questions. If your answer is yes, then you have used prayer to create the future! Furthermore, if you have ever gotten an answer to prayer, then you have operated in the power of God-given imagination. Your prayer created the future!

Reconsider your prayer process in the light of what we've been learning in this book. Your *prayer requests* are actually first creations, and *answers* to your prayer are actually second creations. So, in a very real sense, your prayers create the future!

Please get hold of this. When you lift up a prayer request, you are asking God for something. That "something" is an inner image of what you want to happen, so your prayer request is a first creation. The answer to your prayer is a second creation, something that comes into existence because you prayed, something that wouldn't have happened unless you had prayed. In a very real sense, your prayers create the future.

If you did it once, you can do it again. You simply need to get hold of how the same God who created all things has invited us to be "co-creators" of the future through prayer. It might surprise you to realize that God wants to change the future even more than you do. If it matters to you, it matters to the God who loves you, and He has given you the privilege of being His co-laborer.

"God is a dreamer and He is looking for people who will dream His dreams with Him."
—*Bill Johnson*[24]

When we say you can create the future, the operative word is *create*. So let's take a moment to carefully consider what God's Word says about the creative process.

The Creative Process

The foundational Scripture that explains the creative process that God has built into His creation is found in Hebrews 11:3 (KJV).

> *Through faith we understand that the worlds were framed by the word of God, so that **things which are seen were not made of things which do appear.***

We have already seen how this Scripture confirms the fact that everything is created twice. The process looks like this:

1. The first creation of all things took place within the heart and will of God as He imagined the future and what He desired to happen.

2. By faith, God spoke that image into existence.

3. This produced the second creation, the incarnation of God's imagination, which includes all things that are seen.

24. Bill Johnson, *Dreaming with God: Co-Laboring with God for Cultural Transformation* (Shippensburg, PA: Destiny Image, 2006), xiv.

Again, remember what Berdyaev said: "God created the world by imagination."

I am convinced that this pattern, established by God in creation, applies to us today. I am not the first to believe it. Let's return to Dorothy Sayers, who in her classic book, *The Mind of the Maker*, writes that the creative process by which God made the worlds exactly prefigures the human experience in creating things.

> The point I shall endeavour to establish is that these statements about God the Creator...are not irrelevant to human life and thought. On the contrary...they are, when examined in the light of direct experience, seen to be plain witness of truth about the nature of the creative mind as such and as we know it. So far as they are applicable to man, they embody a very exact description of the human mind while engaged in the act of creative imagination.[25]

Remember that imagination, or the first creation, is indispensable to the creative process, because it must come first. There can be no second creation until there is a first creation. Whenever we see mankind create something, we are looking at man mimicking the God who created all things.

"God created man in His own image and likeness, i.e., made him a creator too."
—Nikolai Berdyaev

---

25. Dorothy Sayers, *The Mind of the Maker*, preface.

In other words, we are never more like God than when we create something![26] Once we grasp the pattern of how God creates, we are ready to understand the power of faith and prayer, and the vital role that our imagination plays in *effectual* prayer, or prayer that changes the future. Remember, every prayer request is a first creation, and every answered prayer is a second creation.

When we go to God in prayer, we are asking for something that does not yet exist to come to pass. Our words of petition are actually images or pictures of a preferred future, one that exists only in our minds and hearts. When we pray, we are expressing a request for a *desired* outcome. This "desire" exists inside of us, in the realm of imagination. So the prayer request comes out of the first creation. Prayer is the articulation of the first creation that is within us, the request for God to make "seen" what is "unseen"; so our answered prayers are actually second creations.

How to Pray a Prayer That Creates the Future

The great proof text for all we are saying is Mark 11:22–23, which is arguably the most famous passage about faith and prayer in the Bible.

> *And Jesus answering saith unto them, Have faith in God. For verily I say unto you, That whosoever shall say unto this mountain, Be thou removed, and be thou cast into the sea; and shall not doubt in his heart, but shall believe that those things which he saith shall come to pass; he shall have whatsoever he saith.*   (Mark 11:22–23 KJV)

---

26. We use the word *create* advisedly. In the strictest sense, only God can create *ex nihilo*, or "out of nothing." When man creates, he is using raw material already provided by God. Nevertheless, at a human level, man can truly be considered a "co-creator" with God. Indeed, this is what we are doing when we pray for things that do not yet exist.

Let's unpack the power of this famous passage of Scripture, line by line.

> *Have faith in God.* (Mark 11:22 KJV)

Or...

> *Have the God kind of faith.*
> (Mark 11:22 KJV, marginal note)

Both translations are accurate, but I like the marginal reading here, because it seems to invite us to operate in the "God kind" of faith, and correctly implies that we have the ability to exercise our faith the same way that God used His. So how does this God kind of faith operate? As we have already seen, God speaks what is inside of Him to create what He desires to see outside of Him. "Speak to the mountain, and it shall be removed." (See Mark 11:23.)

Let's say your desire, or the image inside you, is to see your "mountain" removed. So your prayer request—your dream, desire, or vision of the future—is your first creation. When that "mountain" is actually removed, you have received the answer to your prayer, which is the second creation. You created the future.

The next verse is simply a restatement of the principle even more clearly (with my comments in brackets).

> *Therefore...., what things soever ye desire* [the first creation], *when ye pray, believe that ye receive them* [have faith that your prayer has been heard], *and ye shall have them* [the second creation]. (Mark 11:24 KJV)

Believe, and you shall have.

Moving in the God kind of faith when we pray means that we use the amazing privilege of co-creating the will of God through prayer. We imitate God. We begin with desire, a first creation, that which is not seen. Out of that inner image of what we desire, we pray, believing that the second creation must come to pass and is already ours. The prayer of faith sets supernatural forces at work that change things in the physical world. When the prayer is answered, we have the second creation in the physical realm. We prayed a prayer that creates the future.

Always remember that your hopes, dreams, visions, and imaginations for a preferred future are first creations, the place where prayer begins. Praying effectively requires you to see on the inside (in the present) what you desire to see on the outside (in the future). Getting a revelation of how we can create the future through prayer will ignite our faith to pray more often and more effectively.

The Fourth Dimension

Dr. Paul Yonggi Cho is the pastor of one of the largest churches in the world in Seoul, South Korea. In his classic book, *The Fourth Dimension*, Dr. Cho describes effectual prayer as an "incubation process," and writes about how the things we hope for come to pass in four stages:

1. Envisioning a clear-cut objective.

2. Having a burning desire.

3. Praying for assurance.

4. Speaking the word.[27]

---

27. Dr. Paul Yongi Cho, *The Fourth Dimension: Discovering a New World of Answered Prayer*, vol. 1 (Alachua, FL: Bridge-Logos Publishers, 1979).

Dr. Cho emphasizes the importance of what goes on in our hearts and minds, and shows how incubation takes place in our thoughts. In the light of what we've been saying in this book, he might have called the first two steps the first creation, which is where all answered prayers begin. Cho's "fourth dimension" lies outside the physical world, in the realm of the supernatural, where all things are made possible: "Visions and dreams are the language of the fourth dimension, and the Holy Spirit communicates through them."[28]

The world says, "I'll believe it when I see it." But Jesus says, "If you don't believe it, you'll never see it!" (See, for example, John 16:24.) The believing takes place inside. You must see it first in your heart and mind. Do the work of first creation, praying in faith and believing you have what you see (and what you say), and you will indeed have it as a second creation!

> *Until now you have asked for nothing in My name; ask and you will receive, so that your joy may be made full.*
>
> (John 16:24)

Every true child of God has known the joy of receiving some answer to prayer at some time or another. This is how God designed us to live. So just to make sure you've got this down, take a moment to do this exercise:

1. Pause and think about one particular answer to prayer that you have received from God.

2. Now consciously acknowledge that your answered prayer was a second creation.

3. Think back to the actual prayer(s) you prayed, and realize that something happened even *before* you prayed. That "something" is the subject of this book. You used your imagination!

---

28. Ibid., 31–32.

4. Your imagination was the dream, hope, vision, or desire you had even before you prayed. Indeed, it was the *source* of everything—the first creation.

Answered prayers originate in the imagination as prayer requests; so if you can pray, you are not a victim. And you don't have to wait to get started. You can do the work of first creation right now, because it takes place in your mind and in your heart. Marketplace guru Brian Tracy states the case well in the title of his book: *Create Your Own Future*. He also wrote,

> You must create your desired reality in your mind before you can experience it in your world. And you have complete control over your own mind.[29]

(These quotations from various business books may make some Christians nervous. Sometimes, we are too religious for our own good and reject truth because we fear falling into secular of beliefs of any sort. In many cases, however, you will discover that we are not teaching their stuff; they are teaching our stuff.)

On the other hand, we must pause now to acknowledge the fact that there *are* dangers associated with using the power of imagination. The power of God-given imagination is spiritual dynamite, and it must be handled with care!

---

29. Brian Tracy, *Create Your Own Future* (Hoboken, NJ: Wiley, 2005), 24.

5

WARNING: HANDLE
WITH CARE

Y ou won't find warning labels on a package of cotton balls or a bottle of water. These items are safe to handle. But there are always warning labels on a bottle of pills or a box of dynamite. It is always dangerous to mishandle powerful things—including imagination.

The power of imagination is spiritual dynamite; it is a two-edged sword. Misusing it can hurt you and those you love. While it's true that "imagination is the greatest gift God has given to us,"[30] it is *also* true that "the imaginative faculty, like any other human faculty, can be used for good or evil."[31] Consider this chapter a warning label!

---

30. Oswald Chambers, *My Utmost for His Highest* (Grand Rapids, MI: Discovery House, 2012), February 11.
31. Leanne Payne, *The Healing Presence: Curing the Soul Through Union with Christ* (Grand Rapids, MI: Baker Books, 1989, 1995), 164.

Babylon: The Misuse of the Imagination

As we learned in chapter 1, "God's Amazing Gift to Mankind," one of the first references to the power of imagination in the Bible is shown in a *negative* context. The Babylonians came together to build a city and to make themselves a name. They imagined a utopian "city of man." However, none of their grand imaginations included God, which was their great offense. Throughout the rest of Scripture, from Genesis to Revelation, Babylon is mentioned over two hundred times, and always in a negative context.

Throughout history, Bible commentators have noted how Babylon is consistently set in contrast with Jerusalem, serving as a metaphor for spiritual reality.

+ Jerusalem always represents the City of God, while Babylon always represents the city of man.[32]

+ The New Jerusalem represents the bride of Christ (see Revelation 21:2), while Babylon is the seat of the "*mother of harlots*" (Revelation 17:5).

+ Jerusalem's destiny is to "come down from heaven" (see Revelation 21:10), to serve as the eternal dwelling place of the righteous, while Babylon's destiny is to fall into utter destruction (see Revelation 14:8; 18:2, 21).

God's Primary Problem with Babylon

The key to understanding God's eternal displeasure with the Babylonians is to recognize that the central feature of their city was a tower that would allow them to ascend into heaven by their own effort. Babylon thus became the prototype for all false religious systems that would eventually come

---

32. For more on this topic, read St. Augustine's classic work *The City of God*, written in the fifth century AD.

into the world, because they all would share this one common denominator: the belief that man can get to heaven by his own works.[33]

Out of all the religions on earth, *only* Christianity teaches that man cannot get into heaven by his own merits. There is only one way to heaven—trusting in the finished work of Jesus Christ. This explains the so-called exclusive statements of Jesus: *"I am the way, the truth, and the life: no man cometh unto the Father, but by me"* (John 14:6 KJV).

There is widespread belief that there are many paths to God; that heaven is our destination, and there are many roads to get us there; and that God will eventually accept us as long as we do our best. And these beliefs all sound so wise, loving, and inclusive. But these ideas *imagine* God to be someone other than who He has revealed Himself to be. These statements, as well as what all non-Christian religious systems and sects preach, are just various expressions of the Babylonian imagination.

The world of religion is not nearly as complicated as it may appear. We need to understand that when God looks at the earth, He sees two things: (1) the one and only way to get into heaven through His Son, Jesus Christ, and (2) all the other religions and systems by which man has imagined he can get to

---

33. Babylon is a metaphor for the false religious systems of the world, but political systems can also be Babylonian in nature, especially when God is replaced by the state as the people's deity. Nebuchadnezzar built a golden image of himself and required the people to worship it. (See Daniel 3:1–7.) Adolph Hitler envisioned a new Germany, a Third Reich, that would rule the earth for 1,000 years, in which 6 million Jews were exterminated. Karl Marx re-imagined the nation of Russia, and today this atheistic, socialistic nation is an enemy of the free world. Today, radical Islam imagines a jihad (a "holy war") that will rid the world of Christians and Jews and force all people to live with the evils of terrorism in many forms. The point is that *any* imagined religious or political system without God at the center is Babylonian in nature.

heaven or to a heaven-like state.[34] The reason there is so much confusion in the world about the subject of religion is because God Himself has rendered it so.

> *"Come, let Us go down and there confuse their language, so that they will not understand one another's speech." So the* LORD *scattered them abroad from there over the face of the whole earth; and they stopped building the city. Therefore its name was called Babel, because there the* LORD **confused the language** *of the whole earth; and from there the* LORD **scattered them abroad** *over the face of the whole earth.*
>
> (Genesis 11:7–9)

Notice that God's judgment upon man's misuse of imagination is twofold: He "confuses" and "scatters."

In the same way Babylon prefigures all of man's evil imaginations about how to attain heaven, happiness, and success apart from God, so God's judgment upon them prefigures how He deals with all other false religious systems men have imagined: He confuses and scatters them.

When someone's language is confusing, we say that he is "babbling." That's because the English word *babble* is derived from the term "Babylon," signifying "confusion."

Today, there are literally thousands of religious denominations and sects in the world, and just as many secular systems,

---

34. This view explains the "exclusive" claims of Jesus Christ as being *the* way, *the* truth and *the* life in John 14:6, where He quite clearly states that *"no man can come to the Father but by Me."* God has ordained that faith in Christ is the *only* way to eternal life. Therefore, all other religions of the world are not really "many" in number, they are really just "one" in the same thing, which is summed up in the term *Babylon*. This is why Babylon is called the *"MOTHER OF HARLOTS"* in Revelation 17:5 (KJV). Spiritually speaking, Babylon is the "mother" and source of all the religious systems of the world that offer false ways to heaven apart from Christ.

teachings, and methodologies teaching how to achieve success and happiness. You won't get through any careful study of the first fifty of them without coming away muttering, "Confusion!" And that's because anything man imagines as a means of happiness and joy without God at the center is Babylonian in nature and subject to the judgment of God. He confuses and He scatters.

Babble: to utter sounds or words imperfectly, indistinctly, or without meaning; to talk idly, irrationally, excessively, or foolishly; chatter or prattle.

Mankind's continuing misuse of God-given imagination is not limited to that which is overtly religious. Indeed, the greatest modern-day breeding ground for Babylonian thinking is not found inside of organized religion at all. Welcome to the world of "psychobabble," the idea that you can fix your life by simply changing the way you think, whether God is involved or not.

Today, infomercials and the Internet have flooded us with man-centered misuse of the power of God-given imagination. Millions are made by those who offer success, wealth, and riches by "unleashing the power of the mind," with no mention of God in their message. There is also an abundance of New Age educational material on the power of imagination. However, mishandling our God-given power of imagination is, really, "Old Age," tracing all the way back to Babylon. The common denominator of all these fallacies is always the same—leaving God out.

Think and Grow Rich?

There are a number of good books the world offers to us that are not overtly evil in any way but still don't put Christ at the center of their message. These books can be helpful to us in some ways—the principles they advocate may even be Bible-based—but they include no clear, genuine "warning label" about failing to put God at the center. One primary example of this is the book *Think and Grow Rich* by Napoleon Hill. The theme of the book is, "Whatever your mind can conceive and believe, it can achieve."[35]

Notice that Hill's axiom employs first and second creations. "Whatever the mind of man can conceive" is the first creation; what the mind actually achieves is the second creation. This principle is true, and the book has been a smash. Since its initial publication in 1937, over seventy million copies have been sold worldwide, and it has been ranked the sixth best-selling paperback business book of all time on the *Businessweek* best-seller list. Millionaire businessman W. Clement Stone (1902–2002) was a philanthropist and "New Thought" self-help book author. Stone was a big fan of Napoleon Hill's book, and once commented, "More men and women have been motivated to achieve success because of reading *Think and Grow Rich* than by any other book written by a living author."

The theme of Hill's book has been embraced and practiced by successful people for nearly eight decades. Notable practitioners of the "Think and Grow Rich" philosophy include steel magnate Andrew Carnegie; automobile inventor Henry Ford; and five-and-ten store king F. W. Woolworth; as well as modern achievers like Larry King, broadcaster and comedian; Mary Kay Ash, founder of Mary Kay cosmetics; and Steve Jobs, founder

---

35. Napoleon Hill, *Think and Grow Rich* (Opportunity Informer, 2000, electronic facsimile edition), foreword.

of Apple. Hill's mantra "conceive and achieve" has been para-phrased and restated by others many times and in many forms. "If you can dream it, you can do it" (Walt Disney). "Whatever you vividly imagine, ardently desire, sincerely believe, and enthusiastically act upon must inevitably come to pass" (Jim Harbaugh, head football coach for the University of Michigan).

Notice that all these statements are man-centered. Their emphasis is on what *you* can do. There is no honor given to the great Source of all power.

This Stuff Really Works, But...

I read *Think and Grow Rich* as a young and unsaved high school student, and I distinctly remember what a profound effect it had on my life. I discovered that there really was power in positive thinking. I learned that my attitude would determine my altitude, and I came to realize that even though I couldn't control what happened to me, I could control my *response* to whatever happened to me. I began to apply what I had learned, and experienced some good results. I remember thinking time and again, *Hey, this stuff works!* And it kept working for about ten years. Then, a funny thing happened while I was "thinking and growing rich"—I became a Christian.

After I came to Christ and began to learn the Word of God, it dawned on me that Napoleon Hill's central message left something out. It implied that anyone could achieve success and happiness by harnessing the power of his own mind. But if that was true, who needed God? This is the problem with New Age beliefs, Eastern mysticism, and self-help books. They make the same mistake humanity made when it set about the construc-tion of the Tower of Babel. They leave God out; they effectively take us back to Babylon.

Napoleon Hill's premise, "Whatever your mind can conceive and believe, it can achieve," sounds a great deal like something else: Remember what God said about the Babylonians? *"Nothing they have imagined they can do will be impossible for them"* (Genesis 11:6 AMP).

There is considerable evidence that Napoleon Hill was a Christian. We don't know if he ever read Genesis 11:6, but if he did, he didn't quote it in his book. There are references to a "higher power," but his book never points people to Christ. It's a misuse of imagination, a revisitation of Babylon, and as such, it is profoundly dangerous.

Never underestimate the power of imagination, even evil imagination. It can corrupt a person and even play a part in the defilement of a nation. Let me use the problem of pornography as an example.

The *Playboy* philosophy

The proliferation of pornography and explicit sexual material is widely acknowledged as one of the greatest problems in the world today. Countless lives have been ruined and multitudes of marriages destroyed by its effects. We know that pornography, in one form or another, has been around for centuries, but leave it to America to turn it into an industry. Explicit sexual perversion is on the magazine racks in our bookstores, the screens of our local movie theaters, and a mouse-click away on our laptops. Porn has come out of the closet and gone public. It is everywhere and is readily available, but it wasn't always this way.

I was born in 1944 and grew up in a time in America when you could find pornographic material only if you were determined to look for it. It was out there but wasn't *publicly* out there, because pornography was considered immoral and shameful.

When I was growing up, if you did own any pornography, you'd hide it under the mattress.

Not any more!

Virtually every expression of sexuality is now considered acceptable, and pornography is celebrated as just another expression of free speech. Unless you're an older person like me, you have no real concept of how far our country has fallen away from the traditional family values that sustained previous generations of Americans. Our TV shows have come a long way, from *The Adventures of Ozzie and Harriet*, *Father Knows Best*, and *Little House on the Prairie* to what we see today—*Family Guy*, *Glee*, or *The Bachelor*. This displacement of our national values system didn't happen overnight, but there have been some significant contributing factors that have accelerated its decline. One can be traced to the early 1950s and the imagination of one young man from Chicago, the founding visionary of the *Playboy* magazine empire.

Hugh Marston Hefner was born in 1926. He has described his family as conservative, Midwestern, and Methodist.[36] At age twenty-six, he quit his job as a copywriter for *Esquire* magazine when he was turned down for a five-dollar raise. He raised $8,600 dollars by mortgaging his furniture and acquiring investors, which allowed him to launch *Playboy* magazine. The first issue hit the stands in December 1953, featuring nude photos of Hollywood bombshell Marilyn Monroe. Amazingly, it sold fifty thousand copies. Hefner had gambled that young American males would pay a premium to get hold of nude pictures of famous females, and he won the bet. In selling subsequent issues, he discovered that there was a big market for naked women, whether famous or not.

---

36. Michael Quintanilla, "Pajama Party," *Los Angeles Times* (5 February 1999), http://articles.latimes.com/1999/feb/05/news/cl-4989.

But there was more to *Playboy* magazine than nude pictures.

Playboy's success eventually inspired the creation of competitor magazines like Bob Guccione's *Penthouse* and Larry Flynt's *Hustler,* both of which feature nude pictures. However, *Playboy* was different. Hugh Hefner dreamed about more than just bringing photos of nudity to the men of America; he actually saw himself as a modern-day prophet, a man with a message for his generation. He imagined himself to be the chief advocate and articulator of nothing less than a new, sexually liberated worldview for the young men of America. Nude pictures were the bait; but the real rat poison was in his articles and essays, which encouraged men to cast off the Victorian, puritanical restraints imposed on them by both religion and their parents in order to embrace a new world of sexual freedom. The magazine was the vehicle that carried his message. Hefner called his sexually liberated, hedonistic lifestyle "the *Playboy* philosophy." Those articles and essays sounded radical and disturbing in the 1950s, but today, the corrupting leaven of Heffner's licentious philosophy has worked its way through the whole loaf of American culture. (See Galatians 5:9.) The *Playboy* philosophy has become a way of life for many, and we are worse because of it.

Why pick on *Playboy*?

It is not my purpose to demonize Hugh Hefner. Indeed, there are many things people admire about him, especially as it relates to the subject of this book. For example, he surely used the power of imagination to build an empire. He is a real visionary, and everything he conceived, he achieved. (For all we know, he might have consciously employed the principle set forth in Napoleon Hill's book.) All he imagined came to be, so why pick on *Playboy*?

I'm trying to show you how Hugh Hefner's *Playboy* philosophy, though not connected with the world of organized religion, is really just a revisitation of Babylon. He imagines a world free of the constraints of religion and sexual boundaries—a world without God—resulting in a life of happiness and pleasure.

So it is that Hefner joined the ranks of other men who tried to offer salvation through solutions to life's problems without any involvement of the Deity, or the pesky presence of a Creator God. Friedrich Nietzsche imagined that man's salvation would be realized by embracing his "will to power" and exercising his authority over others, by force if necessary;[37] Karl Marx imagined that man's happiness would be found only when economic issues were solved through the equal distribution of wealth by the state;[38] Sigmund Freud imagined that most of man's fundamental problems were sexually related and that proper psychoanalysis could fix him.[39] The influence of these men is still evident today. They are all the fathers of philosophies that, for the most part, ignore God or do away with Him altogether. Like Hefner's *Playboy* philosophy, they all are just modernized expressions of the age-old Babylonian idea that man can be happy and fulfilled without any involvement with God.

---

37. Friedrich Nietzsche (1844–1900), a German philosopher and cultural critic, advocated man's "will to power," which helps us understand human behavior. His concept *Übermensch* (German for "superman") was said to have influenced Adolf Hitler.
38. Karl Marx (1818–1883) was a German philosopher who believed that human societies progress through class struggle. His *Communist Manifesto* described capitalism as the great evil that should be overthrown by revolutionary action, thus producing a classless society governed by producers. Marx is considered to be one of the most influential figures in human history and is the father of socialistic/communistic systems that do not acknowledge God.
39. Sigmund Freud (1856–1939) was an Austrian neurologist and the founding father of psychoanalysis. Freud believed that faith in God, once necessary to curb societal violence, was no longer needed after advancements in science and reason.

Blank Checks

Isn't it amazing that God has entrusted the spiritual dynamite of imagination to the entire human race, to the sinful as well as to the righteous? You would think that God would limit His distribution of the powerful gift of the imagination only to those who use it for good. But this is not so. Evil men throughout history have used the power of imagination to create evil things; yet God has not withdrawn His gift. On the contrary, God has literally *doubled down* on His promises to grant those of us who know Jesus as Savior *whatever* we can imagine. In Ephesians 3:20, the apostle Paul tells us that God is able to go even further than the furthest we think He can go.

> *Now to* [God] *who is able to do exceedingly abundantly above all that we ask or think, according to the power that works in us....* (Ephesians 3:20 NKJV)

It seems to me that Paul is saying, "Ask! Think! Imagine!" Use the power that is at work within you and know that God "*is able to do exceedingly abundantly above all that*"! What an invitation to be a dreamer!

When someone with unlimited resources wants to extravagantly bless someone, he or she might pull out their checkbook, date it, sign it, and then hand it to that someone who can now write in whatever number they want. The amount written into a signed blank check is not determined or limited by the one who signed it, but by the imagination of the one who fills in the amount.

We all know that the only One in the universe who has completely unlimited resources is God. Some of the most amazing statements in the Bible are those in which God seems to give His people a blank check.

He did it with Solomon. *"The Lord appeared to Solomon in a dream at night; and God said, 'Ask what **you wish** Me to give you'"* (1 Kings 3:5).

And He did it with David. *"Then Nathan said to David, 'Do all that is in your heart, for God is with you'"* (1 Chronicles 17:2 NKJV).

One of David's psalms clearly reveals how he recognized that he had been given a "blank check" from God.

> *O Lord, in Your strength the king will be glad, and in Your salvation how greatly he will rejoice! You have given him his heart's desire, and You have not withheld the request of his lips.*　　　　　(Psalm 21:1–2)

Some of you may be asking yourself, *Wow! How great would it be if someone gave me a blank check?* The very thought of it may send you off imagining the amount you would fill in and what you would buy with the money after cashing the check. The only thing you would need to start such imagining is faith in the one who signed the check!

So I have a question for you: Do you believe in God? Do you believe that He has unlimited resources? Really? Then get ready to start dreaming, because God has not limited His blank checks to Solomon and David; He offers the same gifts to you and me!

Consider the words of Jesus to His disciples in the gospels of Matthew, Mark, Luke, and John:

> *And all things you ask in prayer, believing, you will receive.*　　　　　(Matthew 21:22)

*Therefore I say to you, all things for which you pray and ask
["desire" (KJV)], believe that you have received them, and
they will be granted you.*   (Mark 11:24)

*And I say to you, ask, and it will be given to you; seek,
and you will find; knock, and it shall be opened to you. For
everyone who asks, receives; and he who seeks, finds; and to
him who knocks, it will be opened.*   (Luke 11:9–10)

*If you abide in Me, and My words abide in you, **ask whatever you wish**, and it will be done for you.*   (John 15:7)

*You did not choose Me but I chose you, and appointed you
that you would go and bear fruit, and that your fruit would
remain, so that whatever you ask of the Father in My name
He may give to you.*   (John 15:16)

These promises sound like "blank checks" to me!

If we really believe in the unlimited resources and power of
God, we need to start writing some checks. We need to begin
to imagine the amounts that we would fill in, and dream about
how we'll use the money. This power must be handled with care,
because it is possible to misuse the power of God-given imagination and to mishandle "blank check" promises from God. Jesus'
promises include "whatever we wish" (see John 15:7), "whatever
we desire" (see Mark 11:24 KJV), and "whatever we ask." Did
God really mean it? Isn't this too good to be true? If all this is
true, we may be asking, "What's the catch?"

There's no catch, but there are some qualifiers and warn-
ings. Here are seven guidelines for how to use your God-given
imagination.

Seven Guidelines for God-Given Imagination

#1: Get started: You have to ask!

Reading about the power of God-given imagination in this book without practicing it is like going to the doctor and not getting a prescription filled. The power of imagination won't work unless you use it. The fundamental problem for many of God's people is that they don't write out any checks. They never engage their imagination to fill in the blank. In short, they don't imagine; they don't dream; and they don't pray. Some say, "Nothing happens until someone prays." I have never been able to agree with this because God is sovereign and the Bible is full of things God did without someone's prayer. Blessings come into our lives that we do not pray for. Nevertheless, the most fundamental flaw we find in the church is prayerlessness. James wrote, "*You do not have because you do not ask*" (James 4:2).

Remember, everything is created twice, and only God can bring about the second creation. But only you can conceive the first creation that creates the future.

#2: Check your motives.

The apostle James tells us that our first problem is that we don't ask (see James 4:2), but then he immediately addresses our second problem: "*You ask and do not receive, because you ask with wrong motives, so that you may spend it on your pleasures*" (James 4:3). If you don't ask, you won't receive; but if you ask with a lustful motive, you won't receive anything, either. Check your heart. (More on this in chapter 9.)

#3: Pray according to God's will.

> *This is the confidence which we have before Him, that, if we*
> *ask anything according to His will, He hears us.*
>
> (1 John 5:14)

The greatest obstacle to using our God-given imagination is lack of confidence that we are asking for God's will. You begin to dream, you begin to imagine, but then you give up, stymied by the question "How do I know if what I'm imagining is in line with God's will?" I encourage you to stop overcomplicating things. Trust the Holy Spirit within you. Would a Christian man ever ask God to fulfill his imagination about going to bed with his neighbor's wife? Of course not! If you are a born-again child of God, *trust your inner instinct.* You have the Holy Spirit of God within you, and He will be your Guide. If you *"ask amiss"* (James 4:3 KJV), He will let you know. I am personally convinced that 1 John 5:14 actually guarantees us that we cannot pray for anything outside of God's will with *confidence.* We can fantasize and conjure, but we can be confident in what we are imagining or dreaming only if it's in accordance with God's will. Trust Him!

#4: Practice the presence of God.

Our greatest safeguard against the improper use of our imagination comes with practicing the presence of God. Let us look at two Scriptures that give us confidence to release our imagination without fear.

> *Delight yourself in the* LORD*; and He will give you the*
> *desires of your heart.*　　　　　　(Psalm 37:4)

This is one of my favorite verses in the Bible. It can be interpreted two ways. The traditional interpretation is that, as long as you truly make the Lord your chief delight, you can be sure that the desires of your heart (whatever you can imagine) are what He wants to give you. Lately, however, I've seen another way of looking at it. When you delight yourself in the Lord, you will receive the desires of your heart! In other words, when God is at the center of our life, He Himself creates the very desires we feel. Either way you read it, truly delighting yourself in the Lord is the pathway to a "purified" imagination.

Here is another verse for reminding yourself that your motivations for imaginations and dreams are pure.

> *Trust in the Lord with all your heart and do not lean on your own understanding. In all your ways acknowledge Him, and He will make your paths straight.*
> (Proverbs 3:5–6)

I like to practice the presence of God by "acknowledging" Him at all times. If we continually live in the very presence of God, this verse promises that He will "direct our paths" and be involved in everything we do.

#5: Cast down evil imaginations.

> *…Casting down imaginations, and every high thing that exalteth itself against the knowledge of God.*
> (2 Corinthians 10:5 KJV)

The fact that the apostle Paul addresses the church with these words tells us that Christians are capable of evil imaginations that exalt themselves against the knowledge of God. Even though we are born again, our minds are not totally renewed. Our "old man" is crucified with Christ (see Romans 6:6); but, sometimes, he tries to wiggle off the cross! So when we begin to move out in faith and exercise our imagination, we need to be aware that our hearts can deceive us.

Consider this: *"The heart is deceitful above all things, and desperately wicked: who can know it?"* (Jeremiah 17:9 KJV). Some of you might object to my use of this Scripture, because Jeremiah is obviously describing the condition of the unregenerate, sinful heart. You might argue, quite rightly, that the prophet Ezekiel promised that God would give His people a *"new heart"* (Ezekiel 36:26) under the new covenant.[40]

So why would I warn you about the dangers of a deceitful heart? Because I have seen good Christian people deceived through misuse of the imagination. For a more humorous example, a number of years ago, several women moved to Nashville, Tennessee, and joined our church because they imagined God had told them that they were going to marry famous, single, Christian music celebrities who attended our services. These were Christian women, but they were moving in deception. This is where a good pastor or a faithful friend can lovingly help get such people back on track.

Another subtle form of "evil imagination" is the problem of idolatry in the church. *"Little children, keep yourselves from idols"* (1 John 5:21 KJV). The fact that the apostle John is warning *believers* about idolatry proves that idolatry can be a problem in the church. In this Scripture, John wasn't talking about getting rid of statues. That would be a no-brainer. We need to understand that an idol is anything that has taken the place of the true God in our hearts and minds. We can make an idol out of anything: our spouse, our children, our job, or our material possessions. When we exercise our imagination, we need to make sure that God is on the throne of our hearts. We need to be aware, as

---

40. See also Ezekiel 18:31; 26:36.

John Calvin famously wrote, that "man's nature, so to speak, is a perpetual factory of idols."

Besides making an idol of people or things, idolatry also occurs when we imagine God to be someone/something other than who He has revealed Himself to be. A false image of God is an evil imagination that must be cast down. When you start exercising your God-given imagination, remember to ask the Holy Spirit for discernment.

#6: Learn live in the fear of the Lord.

[God] *grants the desires of those who fear him.*
(Psalm 145:19 NLT)

The psalmist says that God will give us our desires if we fear Him. This implies that when we fear the Lord, we can trust that our imaginations and desires are pleasing to God. But this leads us to ask, what is the fear of the Lord?

Let's start with what it is *not*. To fear the Lord does not mean to live with a sense of fear of God's wrath or anger. It does not mean that you dread the Lord in any way or live with a sense of uncertainty as to how He is going to treat you. That might have been how the Old Testament saints understood the term. However, under the new covenant, the fear of the Lord becomes an expression of love. When we truly love someone, we "fear" hurting them or showing them any dishonor or disrespect. We are concerned with their interest and well-being at all times, and live accordingly. So, to walk in the fear of the Lord means to live with a sense of awe, respect, and great honor for God and the presence of the Holy Spirit at all times.

As the church, we know that God has not given us a spirit of fear (see 2 Timothy 1:7), that perfect love casts out fear (see

1 John 4:18), and that there are over one hundred "fear not" verses in the Bible. We hear these verses quoted so much that Americanized Christianity preconditions us to run from any term containing the word *fear* without the *not*. But the fear of the Lord is a biblical concept!

♦ God commanded us to fear the Lord.

> *You shall fear only the LORD your God; and you shall worship Him and swear by His name.*   (Deuteronomy 6:13)

> [Jesus said,] *"I say to you, My friends, do not be afraid of those who kill the body and after that have no more that they can do. But I will warn you whom to fear: fear the One who, after He has killed, has authority to cast into hell; yes, I tell you, fear Him!"*   (Luke 12:4–5)

> *The fear of the LORD is the beginning of knowledge.*
> (Proverbs 1:7)

> *The fear of the LORD is the beginning of wisdom.*
> (Proverbs 9:10)

♦ We must learn the fear of the Lord, then teach it to our children.

> *Assemble the people, the men and the women and children and the alien who is in your town, so that they may hear and learn and fear the LORD your God, and be careful to observe all the words of this law. Their children, who have not known, will hear and learn to fear the LORD your God, as long as you live on the land which you are about to cross the Jordan to possess.*   (Deuteronomy 31:12–13)

The fear of the Lord prolongs life.   (Proverbs 10:27)

The fear of the Lord are riches, honor and life.
                                          (Proverbs 22:4)

+ The fear of the Lord was an identifying characteristic of the early church.

So the church throughout all Judea and Galilee and Samaria enjoyed peace, being built up; and going on in the fear of the Lord and in the comfort of the Holy Spirit, it continued to increase.   (Acts 9:31)

Teaching the fear of the Lord in depth is beyond the scope of this book. If you want to learn more about this important subject, please read John Bevere's important book, *The Fear of the Lord.* But, for now, let's just take God at His Word. Live in the fear of the Lord. If you do, you can trust that your desires and imaginations will be pleasing to God.

#7: Always remember that God blesses you to be a blessing.

*Now the LORD said to Abram, "Go forth from your country, and from your relatives, and from your father's house, to the land which I will show you; and I will make you a great nation, and **I will bless you**, and make your name great; and so you shall be a blessing."*   (Genesis 12:1–2)

As you begin to imagine, dream, and envision your preferred future, try to keep in mind that it's not all about you! Pastor Bill Johnson comments:

At some point it has to stop being about us long enough to utilize the benefits of being in Christ for the sake of those around us. Such a position gives us unlimited access to the mysteries of God that enable us to touch the needs of a dying world.[41]

Remember that God blessed Abraham and made him great so that he could *be* a blessing. We've seen how God has given us blank checks to fill out and to cash. God wants to grant your wishes and desires. However, let this be the final warning label in this important chapter: While it's OK to ask for a blessing, always remember that your blessing must not end with you. Be sure you "ask" if God has others in mind. It will keep you safe.

Notice that when Jesus taught us how to pray, He used language that implies that whatever we ask from the Lord should come from a corporate mind-set, showing us that the favor and blessing of the Lord will always include the means for directly and indirectly blessing others. Notice that all the personal pronouns in the Lord's Prayer are *plural*!

> *Our* Father...Give *us* this day *our* daily bread. And forgive *us our* debts, as *we* also have forgiven *our* debtors. And do not lead *us* into temptation, but deliver *us* from evil.
>   (Matthew 6:9–13)

It is obviously permissible to ask for yourself, but if you use the "*us*," and "*our*," pronouns in your prayer requests, it will safeguard you from selfishness and from asking amiss.

This is one of the longer chapters in this book because I wanted to drive home the fact that the power of imagination can be misused. However, I also believe that it's time to take back the spiritual dynamite of imagination, which the world has hijacked from the church, and use it to blow up the kingdom of darkness.

---

41. Bill Johnson, *Dreaming with God*, 67.

We must not allow the fear of potential misuse to paralyze its release. As Pastor Bill Johnson aptly notes:

> There is great paranoia over the use of the imagination in the Church of the Western world. As a result, unbelievers often lead the way in creative expression—through the arts and inventions. They have no bias against imagination.[42]

Don't let fear of misusing your imagination stop you. Keep God at the center and practice the principles in both this chapter and chapter 9, "The Activation of Your Imagination." Imagination is dynamite; handle it with care.

---

42. Ibid.

6

LEARNING TO DREAM AGAIN

*And it shall come to pass **in the last days**, saith God, **I will pour out of my Spirit** upon all flesh: and **your sons and your daughters shall prophesy**, and your **young men shall see visions**, and your **old men shall dream dreams**: and on my servants and on my handmaidens I will pour out in those days of my Spirit; and they shall prophesy....*
—Acts 2:17–18 (KJV)

There seems to be a never-ending flow of Christian books and TV shows about what will happen leading up to and during the last days. Some are waiting for the rapture; some are expecting Armageddon; some are trying to figure out the identity of the Antichrist; some are watching for the Great Apostasy. But according to Peter's prophecy in Acts 2, what we ought to be looking for in the days ahead is this:

+ An outpouring of the Holy Spirit.

+ A cross-generational and gender-inclusive move of God— for the *young* men and *old* men, *sons* and *daughters*, and "*servants*" and "*handmaidens.*"

+ An outpouring characterized by its release of God-given imagination in prophecy, dreams, and visions!

I believe that, in our near future, we will see a mighty outpouring of the Spirit of God that will restore our capacity to imagine and to dream. That's what I'm looking for. That's what I'm *expecting* to see.

You need to understand that the power of imagination has everything to do with the future and what you think about it. Imagination creates *expectation*. How you see the future affects how you live in the present. If you see yourself winning in the future, you'll start acting like a winner in the present. If you see yourself losing in the future, you'll start acting and thinking like a loser in the present. Whether you realize it or not, the images inside of you become self-fulfilling prophecies. One author stated it this way: "You are today where your thoughts have brought you; you will be tomorrow where your thoughts take you."[43]

While doing some research for this book, I came across a lot of quotations from American author James Lane Allen, who had a lot to say on our subject. Here are some of his other powerful quotations:

You cannot escape the result of your thoughts.[44]

---

43. James Allen, *As a Man Thinketh and Other Writings* (Stilwell, KS: Digireads.com Publishing, 2005), 33.
44. Ibid.

Whatever your present environment may be, you will fall, remain, or rise with your thoughts, your Vision, your Ideal. You will become as small as your controlling desire; as great as your dominant aspiration.[45]

Allen believed, quite rightly, that our lives are lived "inside out"; the dominant inner images we hold in our hearts determine our future.

The Vision that you glorify in your mind, the Ideal that you enthrone in your heart—this you will build your life by, this you will become.[46]

It's obvious from these quotations that James Allen understood the first and second creations, even if he didn't use that language. He encourages us to dream—and to dream big!

Dream lofty dreams, and as you dream, so you shall become. Your Vision is the promise of what you shall one day be; your Ideal is the prophecy of what you shall at last unveil.[47]

You already know how to do this; but you might have to become more childlike to learn how to do it again!

Recapturing Your Childlike Capacity to Dream

Assuredly, I say to you, whoever does not receive the kingdom of God as a little child will by no means enter it.
(Mark 10:15 NKJV)

---

45. Ibid., 16.
46. Ibid., 17.
47. Ibid., 15.

When Jesus tells us that receiving the kingdom requires child-like qualities, we tend to think in terms of a child's humility, meekness, and faith, overlooking one of the most wonderful qualities in a child—the marvelous capacity to *imagine*. I heard Bill Johnson tell this delightful little story that makes the point perfectly.

A teacher gave her first-grade class students the assignment of drawing a picture of a famous person of their choosing. As the students busily went about the work, the teacher walked through the classroom observing their progress. She noticed one little girl who was really into it, and asked her, "And who are you drawing?"

The little girl replied, "I'm painting a picture of God!"

The teacher was startled. "You can't draw a picture of God, because no one knows what He looks like."

The little girl immediately replied, "They will in a minute!"

"Every child is born blessed with a vivid imagination. But just as a muscle grows flabby with disuse, so the bright imagination of a child pales in later years if he ceases to exercise it."
—Walt Disney

A fertile imagination comes naturally to children. Our little boys dress up like Spiderman and Superman; our little girls become nurturing mothers to their dolls, or dream of being a famous chef or nurse. It's interesting that the images that they act out are always *positive*. No child dreams of becoming a villain or a hobo. You'll never find a child running around saying that he or she wants to grow up to be the village idiot!

Children are delightfully imaginative. Dreaming about a bright future just comes naturally to them. But it has been my observation that, the older children get, the less they use their imagination. Our little girls enter kindergarten imagining themselves to be princesses; but by the time they are in junior high, they allow themselves to be mistreated or disrespected by their boyfriends. Our little boys enter first grade with dreams of becoming astronauts and policeman; but by the time they enter high school, they can't seem to get excited about any kind of career. It's troubling that so many American high schoolers today seem bored, disengaged, or even depressed. The national rate of teen suicide is alarming. What happened to them? Why did they lose excitement about the future? When did the dreamer inside them begin to die?

Autopsy of a Dreamer

When someone dies unexpectedly, the county medical examiner performs an autopsy to determine the cause of death. If the dreamer inside the imagination of our children has died, maybe we ought to perform a spiritual autopsy to find out why.

I would suggest that the primary problem often begins in our homes. I believe that we, as parents, might be to blame for the demise of our children's ability to dream. Obviously, we don't mean to do it. Unconsciously, we smother their capacity to dream in our misguided attempts to prepare them for the real world. We know from experience that many dreams don't come true. So when we hear our children start dreaming out loud about some wonderful (though logically impossible) preferred future, we find ourselves telling them, "Don't get your hopes up." We may think we are helping our children, cushioning their little souls to better absorb the blows of life's disappointments, but we are actually harming them by discouraging their capacity to dream.

Perhaps we do this because we haven't understood how our own disappointments in life have robbed us of our personal ability to dream, unconsciously projecting our pessimism onto our children. Don't do this! If your children begin to dream out loud about what they would like their future to look like, even if it sounds far-fetched or unrealistic, go ahead and encourage them. You don't have to appoint yourself as their "Dream Deputy" or "Soul Sheriff," shooting down every imagination that sounds unrealistic to you. It's so easy to slip into the role of discourager of our children's dreams.

We can be guilty of the same thing in our marriages. For example, the other day, my wife, Elizabeth, reminded me once again that even before we got married, she had always wanted to be hairdresser, but she'd never pursued it because I'd discouraged her. Whoa—what a wake-up call! We've been married for forty-seven years, and even though I heard her mention this many times, I don't ever remember having a really *serious* discussion about it. Upon reflection, I remembered that when she would talk about her feelings about going to cosmetology school, I never really encouraged her. In my mind, I immediately dismissed the idea as unrealistic. My reasoning was all negative. I was fixated on all the realities: we had young children, I had a full-time job, school would cost money we didn't have, and so forth. The bottom line was that, in my own mind, I just couldn't "see" her doing that. So it never happened. Now, whether or not cosmetology school was God's best for her is arguable. Maybe she wouldn't have done it even if I had encouraged her. We'll never know. The point is that I'm not proud of my negative response. You might even say that I killed her dream.

In my defense, I can honestly say that this has not been a pattern in my life. On the contrary, I have always been very careful not to stomp on anyone's dream, even if it sounds implausible or unlikely to happen. The seedbed of my own imagination was well watered when I was a child, and it's never been my style to walk carelessly through someone else's "garden." Long before I came to believe in God, I believed in the power of imagination. Looking back, I'm convinced that God was preparing me to write this book from my early childhood. His amazing grace filled me with a profound appreciation for the power of imagination, even before I knew He had authored it! Here's my story.

My journey into the theater of the mind

I have always loved to read. Many boys don't. I remember talking to my dad about my passion for *reading*, and he said that he knew exactly where it had come from. Dad told me how, almost from infancy, my mom would sit me on her lap and read to me by the hour. He said that I would dramatically protest when she tried to stop. So I truly believe that my passion for reading started in my mother's lap. I know now that the words she read to me were forming pictures in my mind, which is how I got hooked. My little imagination was at work, fueled by the wonders of reading.

And then, there was the radio. We didn't get our first TV until I was nine, so before then, our entertainment was the radio. My father worked for the Southern Pacific Railroad and was gone a lot. So, in the evening, my Mom, my brother, and I would listen to the radio—and not just to music. The evening programs in those days included dramas like *Gang Busters*, *The Shadow*, and *Gunsmoke*; adventure programs like *Sky King*; mysteries like *Inner*

Sanctum Mysteries; or comedies like *Fibber McGee and Molly* and *My Friend Irma*. One of my favorites was *Lux Radio Theatre*, a classic program that featured current and upcoming movies dramatized for radio. ("Lux" was a brand of soap.) This may sound super dull to you, but I assure you that we were totally entertained. As the actors read through the scripts and the producers added the sound effects, I could actually visualize the scenes in my mind. I loved it. When we got our first TV, I was less than impressed. There were only three channels, the pictures were black-and-white, and the images were snowy. I preferred the radio. Looking back now, I understand why. Because radio had no pictures, it put my imagination to work. It was the "theater of the mind."

My younger brother, Kenny, and I also loved baseball and would listen to the radio broadcasts whenever we could. Those play-by-play announcers were so good that their descriptions

> "Radio is the theatre of the mind. That's its appeal; it is the theater of the mind and of the imagination."
> —Orson Welles[48]

---

48. To understand the power of radio as "the theater of the mind," the reader is invited to research the events of October 31, 1938, when Orson Welles' Mercury Theatre company produced a dramatic adaptation of H. G. Wells' *War of the Worlds* for the radio. Wells' story of a Martian invasion of earth was broadcast live on that Halloween night. The first two-thirds of the one-hour broadcast was written as a series of live radio news bulletins describing the Martian invasion. Many listeners who tuned in after the program had already begun mistook the play for an actual news broadcast, which provoked widespread panic across the country. Telephone switchboards were jammed, electrical circuits were overloaded, and many people abandoned their homes. The event has been studied ever since as an example of the power of imagination in provoking hysteria.

made you feel like you were actually at the game. Baseball is a game of anticipation, and those guys knew how to extract every drop of suspense from any play. They'd have you hanging on every pitch. Eventually, we got around to making up our own games, using the actual lineups from our favorite Major League teams. Using a broom stick as a bat and a red sponge rubber baseball (which wouldn't break the neighbors' windows), we'd go right through all nine innings, with me describing the game out loud as we played, just as if I were a play-by-play announcer on the radio. We might have been in the backyard of our family residence in Lake Charles, Louisiana; but, in our minds, we were at Yankee Stadium in New York. It all seemed so real to us!

And finally, of course, there was the movie theater. We grew up watching cowboy movies starring Roy Rogers, Gene Autry, and William "Hopalong Cassidy" Boyd. Heroic images of the "good guys" stamped powerful images in our minds. When we played, we'd strap on our little guns and holsters and act out our own movies, mowing down the bad guys with our cap pistols. Of course, we had to take turns being the hero, because, in our minds, the good guys wore white hats and always won. A generation later, our little boys would swap their cap pistols for lightsabers and pretend to be Luke Skywalker.

Nothing much really changes. Imagination runs wild in our little children; but, by the time they are mature adults, it's been safely tucked away in a cage—and we, the older generation, were the zookeepers.

Don't let that be your story!

If the primary "dream killer" inhabits our homes in the form of overly practical guardians, the second certainly stalks the catacombs of our culture. As an American, it's hard to remember a time when it's been more difficult to feel good about our future. Our national debt is taking us into a death-dive. Radical Islamic terrorists are taking over the Middle East, vowing to annihilate the nation of Israel and fly the flag of Allah over the White House. Iran is on the verge of acquiring a nuclear weapon, and both our Republican and Democratic politicians seem powerless to do anything. There is a lot of instability in our culture, with so many people finding themselves in seasons of occupational transition and feeling both fear and uncertainty about the future. Over the past thirty years, I have found myself ministering to many brokenhearted, hurting people. Increasingly these days, I find myself giving the same counsel over and over: "You've got to start dreaming again!" The truth is that nothing is more tragic than suffering the death of a dream.

Les Misérables

Over twenty years ago, Elizabeth and I saw the musical *Les Misérables*[49] on Broadway. The 1935 (non-musical) film adaptation of the Victor Hugo novel is one of our favorite movies of all time. However, to see the story set to music was also an amazing experience. The 2012 movie version won an Academy Award for its excellence and is embedded with the Christian themes of grace and sacrificial love. I have to admit that I have never listened to the lyrics of "I Dreamed a Dream" without weeping. A young mother in desperate conditions singing that life has killed the dream she dreamed—even when I watch the movie with others, and don't want them to see a grown man cry, I end up weeping, and I've noticed that I'm not the only one with eye moisture.

I've thought a lot about this song and why it moves us like it does, and I think I've got the answer: *It's because there is nothing*

---

49. The book, play, and film versions of the Victor Hugo novel still use the French title *Les Misérables*, because the term has never been successfully translated into English. Attempts to translate "Les Misérables" into English have resulted in "The Miserable Ones," "The Dispossessed," or, simply, "The Miserable."

sadder or more tragic than broken dreams! This song reconnects us with our own personal experiences of disappointment, broken dreams, and the cruelties of life. I might paraphrase the message of the closing two lines of the song this way: Life has a way of killing the dreams we dream!

The truth is that, as we learned in chapter 3, "The Sustaining Power of Imagination," life is difficult. We all suffer betrayals of trust and devastating disappointments along the way. We make bad decisions and suffer the consequences. Coping with a sense of loss is bad enough, but when these experiences rob us of our ability to dream or to imagine a great future, we suffer the worst loss of all.

Learning from Langston

A while back, I came across a powerful little poem by Langston Hughes that really captures the importance of holding on to your dreams. "Hold fast to dreams," the poem pleads.[50] Hughes really nails it with this poem. If we don't hold fast to our dreams, life is like a "broken-winged bird that can't fly," a "barren field frozen in snow." In yet another poem, he wonders about what happens when a dream is deferred. "Does it dry up / Like a raisin in the sun?"[51] Reading these two powerful poems made me want to know more about the poet. Here's what I found.

Langston Hughes was an American poet, novelist, and playwright whose African-American themes made him a primary contributor to the Harlem Renaissance of the 1920s. Hughes knew something about disappointment and heartbreak. His

50. Langston Hughes, *The Collected Works of Langston Hughes: Works for Children and Young Adults: Poetry, Fiction, and Other Writing*, vol. 11 (Columbia, MO: University of Missouri Press, 2003), 52.
51. Langston Hughes, *The Collected Works of Langston Hughes: The Poems: 1951–1967*, vol. 3 (Columbia, MO: University of Missouri Press, 2001), 74.

parents separated soon after he was born, and his father moved away. Due to his mother's many moves, Hughes was primarily cared for by his maternal grandmother, Mary, but she died when he was in his early teens. It was during these years that Hughes began to dream of being a poet, and he submitted his poems to a number of publishers, with no success. After graduating high school and dropping out of college, he worked as a dishwasher and busboy, and eventually became a steward on a freighter that took him to Spain and Africa. Then he got his breakthrough.

American poet Vachel Lindsay liked Hughes' work, befriended him, and helped him get his poems in front of a larger audience, which landed him a scholarship at Lincoln College. While at Lincoln, he had another friend who used his connections with Knopf Publishers to print Hughes' first book of poetry, *The Weary Blues*, published in 1926. More poetry, novels, and an autobiography followed, and his popularity continued to grow.

> Langston Hughes, one of the leaders of the early 1900s Harlem Renaissance, pushed the "black experience" beyond segregation and discrimination—from the back of the bus to the front of the anthologies. His poems are read and enjoyed in classrooms throughout the country to this day. So pervasive has been the influence of his work [that] the line…"a raisin in the sun" [from his poem "Harlem"] became the title of the acclaimed play by Lorraine Hansberry.[52]

---

52. Arthur Christopher Schaper, "Poetry Analysis: 'Dream Deferred' by Langston Hughes," *The Epoch Times* (5 September, 2012), http://www. theepochtimes.com/n2/arts-entertainment/poetry-analysis-dream-deferred-by-langston-hughes-288523.html. The 1961 movie version of "Raisin In the Sun" is highly recommended.

Langston Hughes' dream of making a difference through his writings eventually came true. He held on to his dream. He knew how to overcome the temptation to give up and how to hang on. He refused to let life kill his dream.

Dare to Start Dreaming Again!

There are so many angry, unhappy, disgruntled, and depressed people these days. Maybe you're one of them. Perhaps you are suffering because of a broken dream or hopes that have been put on hold. It's really a form of mental illness. King Solomon said it this way: *"Hope deferred makes the heart sick"* (Proverbs 13:12 NKJV).

To lose hope and stop dreaming is to lose everything. We ought to encourage one another to cling to the inner image of what life coaches call our preferred future. Too many believers have never realized that their "inner world" has the power to transform their "outer world." We cannot always control what happens to us, but we can control our *response* to what happens to us. We can hold on to our hope. *"We…lay hold upon the hope set before us: which hope we have as an anchor of the soul, both sure and steadfast…."* (Hebrews 6:18–19 KJV).

"The future belongs to those who believe in the beauty of their dreams."
—Eleanor Roosevelt

We can *"lay hold"* of the hope, or the dream of what the future will look like, set before us. That hope will be an *"anchor"* for our souls, *"sure and steadfast."* Believe in your dream.

What Do We Believe the Future Holds for the Church?

This book is addressed to individual believers; but I cannot close this chapter without expanding our focus from the belief of the individual to the belief of the people of God. What we believe together as the people of God affects what is going on in our country. While we have been learning how the power of imagination can transform our *personal* world, we need to recognize that there is also a *corporate* application of the power of imagination that applies to all of us as members of the church of Jesus Christ.

For example, author James Allen famously wrote this about us as individuals: "The outer conditions of a person's life will always be found to reflect [his] inner beliefs." What applies to us as individuals is also true of us as a *group*. In general, the outer condition of the American church today is just a reflection of individual inner beliefs of the body of Christ.

When we take an honest look at the moral and spiritual condition of our country, I think it's fair to say that we as the church are not winning the "culture wars" and impacting society as an agent of change as we know we should. I am convinced that the real problem is not what is going on *around* us but what is going on *within* us. Like the character Pogo from the comic strip, we may wake up one day to find that the real enemy is not "out there" but inside *us*.

We have clearly demonstrated how what an individual believes about his future affects his present. If you believe you are going to lose in the future, you will think and act and make decisions like a loser in the present. Furthermore, the same principle that applies to an individual believer also applies to a group of believers. What we as the body of Christ believe as a group will come to pass. If we truly believe that we will not win the culture wars; if we cannot imagine ourselves as agents of God that can turn the nation around; if we cannot see the church of Jesus prevailing against all the powers of darkness—then we won't!

Eschatology matters

Eschatology is the branch of theology that refers to what we believe the Bible says about the future—the "end times" or the "last days." All Christians believe they will go to heaven, but what do they believe the future on planet Earth will look like before the second coming?

Opinions abound on this subject within the body of Christ, but let me simplify things by saying that we are either optimistic or pessimistic about what the future holds for the gospel and the church in the days to come. This is an important topic, because what we believe about the future affects how we act in the present.

For example, if we really believe we are going on vacation in June, we'll start planning for it earlier in the year. We'll mark the dates off on our calendar. We'll start planning our travel itinerary and setting aside some money for the trip. We'll think about it when we're shopping, purchasing clothing and other items we think we'll need for our holiday. Best of all, we'll get a little "lift" in our soul when we think about it, because we're anticipating a good time. Our eschatology about our future vacation is optimistic as we live in and act out the present according to our belief.

On the other hand, if you time-traveled back to April 1912 onboard the *Titanic*, a ship you knew was doomed to sink, you would have a pessimistic view of the future. You wouldn't be playing shuffleboard. If you were a crewman, you wouldn't be spending time polishing brass or arranging deck chairs. If you believed that the ship was going to go down in the end, why would you engage in something you knew wouldn't really make a difference?

Unfortunately, the present-day Christian church in America is generally pessimistic about the future. Too many of us think we're on the *Titanic*, and we act accordingly. I am convinced that this is why so many Christians don't vote, don't speak out, and don't engage the culture for righteousness' sake. They are expecting things to get worse, because they can't imagine things really getting better, which becomes a self-fulfilling prophecy. Our nation's current condition is the result of what we have believed it would be.

American culture has been in a moral free fall since the 1960s. Prayer has been banned from public schools since 1962. In January 2015, over 57.7 million babies had been aborted since the *Roe v. Wade* Supreme Court decision in 1973.[53] The national debt is moving toward twenty trillion dollars, and we keep electing public officials who don't do anything about it. The Internal Revenue Service is waging an all-out war on Christian churches and ministries, and gay marriage has now been made legal throughout the country. So where is the church?

The sleeping giant

The church is God's "sleeping giant." Just think of the numbers. In 2012, 77 percent of America's population, just over 314 million, claimed to be Christian.[54] In 2013, less than 3 percent of the population self-identified as LGBT.[55] Less than 1 percent

---

53. Steven Ertelt, "57,762,169 Abortions in America Since Roe vs. Wade in 1973," LifeNews.com, January 21, 2015, http://www.lifenews.com/2015/01/21/57762169-abortions-in-america-since-roe-vs-wade-in-1973/.
54. Frank Newport, "In U.S., 77% Identify as Christian," Gallup, December 24, 2012, http://www.gallup.com/poll/159548/identify-christian.aspx.
55. Brian W. Ward, et al., "Sexual Orientation and Health Among U.S. Adults: National Health Interview Survey, 2013," National Health Statistics Reports, no. 44 (Hyattsville, MD: National Center for Health Statistics), 2014, http://www.cdc.gov/nchs/data/nhsr/nhsr077.pdf.

of Americans are Muslim.[56] A 2012 Pew Research Center poll revealed that 5.7 percent of the American population are atheist or agnostic.[57]

If these statistics are reasonably accurate, then professing Christians outnumber the combined total number of atheists, agnostics, LGBT identifiers, and Muslims in this country by more than seven to one, and yet, the church seems to be losing every battle in the culture wars.

What's wrong with this picture?

The prevailing eschatological view of the American church has been one of defeat instead of victory. We as a people do not truly believe that we will win.

Remember, how you see the future affects the present. What you believe about what's coming will influence your thought processes, your decisions, and how you spend your time. We know that most of the 225 million professing Christians in America have a pessimistic view of the future because they're not engaged in the present culture wars! They can't imagine that they could make a difference; therefore, they don't.

A funny thing happened to me on the way to the rapture...

Jesus answered and said to him, "Most assuredly, I say to you, unless one is born again, he cannot see the kingdom of God."   (John 3:3 NKJV)

The church has focused more on being born again than on seeing the kingdom of God.

---

56. Frank Newport, "In U.S., 77% Identify as Christian."
57. Pew Research Center, "'Nones' on the Rise," October 9, 2012, http://www. pewforum.org/2012/10/09/nones-on-the-rise/.

Don't get me wrong. To be born again is an important thing. In one sense, it is the main thing. But Jesus mentioned the term "born again" only once in the four Gospels. In contrast, He used the term "kingdom of heaven," or "kingdom of God," over one hundred and twenty times in the Gospels, and over forty times in Matthew alone! So, how have we missed this?

A number of years ago, as I was meditating on John 3:3, I heard the Holy Spirit say this to me: "Notice that Jesus didn't say *if* you are born again, you *will* see the kingdom; He said *unless* you are born again, you *cannot* see it."

That flash of revelation changed my life. I suddenly understood that it is possible to be born again and still not see the kingdom as a *present* reality.

I was saved in 1971, but I didn't "see" the kingdom of God until 1981. During the first ten years of my walk with Christ, I was taught that the great (future) hope of the church was to be "raptured," or taken away, by Christ before the great tribulation. We were reading all the best-selling books about the imminent return of Christ for His church, and were taught that the increasing evil in the world was proof that the great tribulation, or our "great escape," was close at hand. The prevailing theme of the books we read and the sermons we listened to were not predictions of Christian victory but forecasts of increasing defeat. We were taught that things would get worse and worse but that we could be happy because Jesus was going to come back to rescue us before things got too bad.

The imagery of the future of the church went something like this:

+ We can expect to see many fall away from the faith.

+ Don't be surprised to see the church suffer increasing defeat and persecution, even with a "remnant" remaining faithful to the end.

+ We can all look forward to confronting the eternity-determining decision of whether we will receive the mark of the beast.

+ Expect world conditions to gradually worsen to the point that nearly the whole world will be following the Antichrist and his prophet.

+ Get ready for great tribulation to come upon the earth, but don't worry: Jesus will come back to rapture us into heaven before things get bad.

Some of you reading this book still have this image of what the future of the church will look like. That's what I was taught for the first ten years of my Christian journey. Then a funny thing happened to me. I began to read my Bible and learn about the gospel of the kingdom. Gradually, new images of the future of the church began to form in my mind. For example...

+ Jesus won't return until "all His enemies are under His feet." (See Psalm 110:1; Acts 2:34–35; 1 Corinthians 15:24–25; Hebrews 1:13; Hebrews 10:12–13.)

+ All things promised by the prophets and the restitution of all things must come to pass *before* the return of Jesus. (See Acts 3:19–21.)

+ Jesus is returning for a *"glorious church without a spot or wrinkle or any other blemish"* (Ephesians 5:27 NLT).

+ Light *always* overcomes darkness (see John 1:4–5), and good *always* overcomes evil (see Romans 12:21).

- The kingdom of God is "now" (present reality) with a "not yet" (to be completed in the future) component. The kingdom first came with Christ, and will continue to increase until its final manifestation at the second coming. (See Matthew 3:2; 4:17; 10:7; Mark 1:15; Luke 11:20; 17:20–21; 21:31; Revelation 12:10.)

- The kingdom of God is not the same thing as heaven! The kingdom is the will of God *"done on earth as it is in heaven"* (Matthew 6:10 NKJV)!

- Jesus brought the kingdom from heaven to earth, and there is no end to its increase! (See Isaiah 9:6–7.)

God is in the process of replacing the church's eschatology of defeat with an eschatology of victory. More and more believers are studying the Scriptures referenced above and are beginning to believe that Christ is coming back for a prevailing church and a glorious bride clothed in victory, not defeat. However, until we see victory on the *inside*, we won't see it on the *outside*.

Preachers are fond of declaring, "I've read the back of the book, and we win!" Invariably, the congregation responds with laughter, applause, and a mighty amen! But I wonder if we really believe it.

What is your image of the future of the church? Will she end up battered and defeated, just trying to hold on until the rapture? Or do you see here as a glorious church, emerging triumphant with the power of the gospel? However you see it is how you will live. It's time to allow the Word of God to paint images of future victory and triumph for His church inside you. It will change the way you think, plan, and make decisions. It will change your life; and, by extension, we will change the culture!

In the Mind of God,
the Game Is Already Over

In the mind of God, who knew the end before the beginning, the game is already over.

My son Todd and I like sports, but our ministry schedules often conflict with the ball games we want to watch, so we record them on our DVRs to watch later. However, here's where we are different: When I know I'm recording a game to watch later, I don't want to know the final score before I get a chance to watch it; on the other hand, even though he's taping the game, Todd wants to know the final score as soon as he can get it. Lately, I've been thinking about how our different preferences affect how we watch the game. Occasionally, someone will blurt out the final score of a game I haven't watched yet, and I get upset because I want to watch the recording of the game with the suspense of not knowing the outcome.

However, the other day, I realized that, even though I prefer to watch the recording without knowing the score, there are advantages to knowing the final score ahead of time, especially if my team wins! When I watch a pre-recorded game knowing the final score, my reactions to all the plays are different from what they would be if I didn't know the final score ahead of time. If I know that my team won the game, I won't be discouraged or downcast if my team falls way behind at times. If we make a boneheaded play, it won't shake me because, after all, I know that my team won. In other words, my "eschatology" about how the game ends determines how I interpret the game as I watch it. If I were in suspense about the outcome of the game, I would get really frustrated if my team fumbles the ball or throws an interception; but if I know that we won the game ahead of time, a fumble or interception won't bother me. As a matter of fact, every misstep would only increase my excitement to see how we would eventually win the game anyway!

I know that the church will win in time and history. I know that the gospel of the kingdom will prevail and that all *"the earth will be filled with the knowledge of the glory of the* Lord, *as the waters cover the sea"* (Habakkuk 2:14 nkjv).[58] The Word of God has painted images of victory inside of me. So when I see the world get darker, or the church decline, it's like watching my team have a bad inning in a game I know that we have already won. God will not allow the unbelief of a backsliding generation to thwart His glorious plan to expand His kingdom throughout the earth. He has time to wait on a generation that will believe Him.

It is widely recognized that, up until about one hundred and fifty years ago, the prevailing eschatology in the church was optimistic. The pessimistic view of the future swept through the American church with the widespread acceptance of the doctrine of dispensationalism (the belief that God *changes* the way He relates to human beings depending on the period of history in which they are born) and the adoption of the doctrine of cessationism (the belief that the office gifts of apostle and prophet ceased with the twelve apostles). No wonder the dream of victory for the gospel and the church almost died!

However, the tide is turning. The church is learning to dream again. She has to. In Acts 2, Peter said that it would. So let us expect to see an outpouring of the Holy Spirit marked by the reawakening of dreamers and visionaries! *That* is what we should be looking for!

---

58. See also Numbers 14:21; Isaiah 11:9.

7

CHANGING FROM THE INSIDE OUT

As [a man] *thinks in his heart, so is he.*
—Proverbs 23:7 (NKJV)

Everything is created twice. Whatever is going on in the unseen world of our mind and heart is the key to understanding what is going on around us.

How we think, which is the first creation, determines how we live in everyday life, which is the second creation. What we see comes out of what we cannot see. How you see yourself on the inside, your "self-image," has the power to shape your life on the outside. What you think of yourself on the inside is how you will become on the outside. Therefore, authentic change and real transformation in the kingdom of God always comes from the inside out.

Your inner image of yourself is not only shaping your present and your future, but it also influences those who are close to you.

A Poor Self-Image Kept Israel Out of the Promised Land

God brought the Israelites out of Egyptian bondage by His mighty hand. He brought them to the banks of the Jordan River within a few days. There, on the border of their Promised Land, they hesitated. Instead of entering in, they chose twelve leaders to go ahead of them to spy out the land. Ten of the twelve spies brought back an evil report of unbelief, that, although it was a good land, they believed that they would not be able to possess it because of the giants who dwelled there. However, it wasn't really the giants that kept them out; it was their own poor self-image. Look carefully at what they said:

> So they gave out to the sons of Israel a bad report of the land which they had spied out, saying, "The land through which we have gone…is a land that devours its inhabitants; and all the people whom we saw in it are men of great size. There also we saw the Nephilim [the giants]…and we became like grasshoppers in our own sight, and so we were in their sight."   (Numbers 13:32–33)

Notice that the evil report of the ten spies came out of a poor self-image! They saw themselves as "*grasshoppers*," and they believed that was how the giants saw them, too! How you see yourself is how you think others see you, and you will live according to that self-image.

On the other hand, God saw Israel as His "*church in the wilderness*" (Acts 7:38 KJV), the hope of the nations, but these leaders saw themselves as losers—too weak to walk in all that God had promised them. In other words, the poor self-image of ten men doomed three million people to forty years of wandering in the desert, causing an entire generation to die in the wilderness! (See Numbers 14:30–35.)

So it is today. When the church of the living God imagines itself as small, weak, and helpless in the face of its (giant) enemies, it falls far short of what God promised us we would be—His "*holy nation*" (Exodus 19:6 KJV; 1 Peter 2:9 KJV). It's the responsibility of church leaders and pastors to give a "good report" of faith to God's people, reminding them of their true identity in Christ and encouraging them to cling to the surety of the promises God has made to us. Building a healthy self-image in the children of God is critical, because "*as* [a man] *thinks in his heart, so is he*" (Proverbs 23:7 NKJV).

A poor self-image can keep you out of *your* Promised Land.

Transformation from the Inside Out

What you think in your heart is your first creation. The result, how you live and make decisions, is the second creation. What you think of yourself really matters!

Back in the early 1970s, when I got saved, I lived in Little Rock, Arkansas, and often went shopping at the University Mall. J. C. Penney, Sears, Montgomery Ward, and M. M. Cohn were the anchor stores. M. M. Cohn was the nicest, or most expensive, store in the mall—the place where people shopped for high-end clothing. It was also the store we least visited.

During that time, as a young believer, I read my Bible every day and learned about my new identity in Christ. One day, as I was walking past Cohn's on my way to Sears to buy a shirt, I heard a still, small voice ask me a question: "Why don't you shop for the shirt *here?*" The voice was so clear that I remember stopping in my tracks to hear more—but nothing else came. All I kept hearing was "Why do you never buy anything at M. M. Cohn?" I had a sense that God was asking me a question but He wasn't giving me an answer. So I started asking myself, *Why don't you shop at Cohn?* As I pondered the question, it dawned on me that I simply didn't "see" myself as a Cohn customer. I began to realize that my self-image allowed me to shop at Sears, Montgomery Ward, and J. C. Penney but *not* at M. M. Cohn. My unspoken perspective was, *That store is where the rich people shop, so it's not for me!* I began to realize that the real issue wasn't where I bought my shirts; it was how I saw myself, and the Lord was challenging me to change the way I saw myself.

The next time I went to the University Mall, I made a point of walking through M. M. Cohn. I slowly wandered through the men's department, looking at all the fine, expensive clothes, admiring the exquisite merchandise, and even imagining myself wearing it. I didn't buy anything. I just started thinking about buying something there.

That was the beginning of a pretty amazing transformation of my self-image over the next few months. In subsequent trips to the mall, I always went through Cohn, and eventually, I actually started buying some things there. Over the course of time, my wardrobe underwent a pretty dramatic upgrade. People began to notice, and I was getting a lot of compliments on my new look. I was in sales at the time, and believe me, how you dress *does* make a difference in the marketplace and the corporate world. (More on this in chapter 10, "Serving the Purpose of God in Your Generation," where I recommend John Malloy's classic book *Dress for Success*.) I began to feel better about myself; I began to notice that, in general, people were more respectful to me and seemed to take me more seriously; and, best of all, my sales went up!

The point I am trying to make is that the outer "me" didn't undergo a transformation until the inner "me" changed. I had seen myself as *unworthy* of buying something at M. M. Cohn. My inner image disqualified me from walking through that store, much less actually buying something there. From that experience, I learned that how we see ourselves on the inside determines how we act, react, dress, talk, shop, and make decisions. It's a law: How you think you are is how you are!

God Cares about Our Self-worth!

Let's get this straight. God doesn't care *where* you shop! That was never my point. God asked me the question because He wanted to show me that I was suffering from a poverty mentality and a poor self-image. The Lord wanted me to see myself as His beloved son and to discover that He had made me worthy of enjoying a better shirt if I wanted one.

I realize that some of you may be offended that I used consumerism as an example of the power of our inner image. I assure you that nobody loves a bargain more than I do. I shop a lot at Costco and avidly clip coupons. To this day, I rarely go shopping at Neiman Marcus or Saks Fifth Avenue, because there's limit on what I'm willing to pay for a shirt. Their clothing is highly priced because of the name brands, but it really isn't much better than the high-quality merchandise I can purchase at less expensive stores. However, God taught me an important lesson from this little exercise, and from that time forward, I never considered myself unworthy of wearing *any* shirt or shopping at *any* store.

Many of God's precious people have low self-esteem and identity issues, and see themselves as poor or unworthy of blessing. They still find their self-worth from others instead of from the Word of God. Their "image" of the Father God is still connected to their image of their earthly fathers, which is often a negative image, and their self-worth is still based on what others say about them. They don't realize that the world around them will change only when they change the world *within* them.

Transformation always occurs from the inside out. We live our lives, make our decisions, and plan for our future according to the dominant inner images inside of us. What we are "beholding" on the inside becomes who and what we are on the outside. Indeed, this is how we become more like Jesus.

We Become What We Behold

We become what we behold.

> *But we all, with unveiled face, beholding as in a mirror the glory of the Lord, are being transformed into the same image from glory to glory, just as by the Spirit of the Lord.*
>
> (2 Corinthians 3:18 NKJV)

All true believers want to be more like Jesus, but sometimes we set about it the wrong way. We try to add this or eliminate that. We think we need to change, but what we really need is to be transformed. At the risk of oversimplification, let me express the idea this way: Change is something *you* can do; transformation is something only *God* can do. I can change my clothes, I can change my sheets, I can change my eating habits, and I can even change my spiritual habits; but I can't change *me*—only God can do that. That's why the apostle Paul didn't use the word *changed* in the text. He used the word "*transformed.*" The Greek word for "transformed" in the text is *metamorphoo*, from which we get English word *metamorphosis*.

Metamorphosis: change of physical form, structure, or substance especially by supernatural means.[59]

Religion is often concerned just with externals, but personal transformation takes place from the inside out. The apostle Paul tells us that beholding the glory of the Lord changes us. The metaphor Paul uses teaches us that, when we read the Bible, we look into a mirror and behold images that the Word creates in our minds. As you behold the Lord and who you are in Christ in the unseen realm of your heart, the Holy Spirit does the miracle of transforming you into the image you are beholding, taking you from *"glory to glory."* Notice that this work is done *"by the Spirit of the Lord,"* not by human effort. The work of transformation is supernatural. It's not something we do; it's something God does. We do play a part in the miracle—we must do the work of beholding the inner images formed by the Word of God. Then the Holy Spirit does the rest.

Religion gives us an endless list of dos and don'ts and teaches us to try harder to be more like Jesus. But true transformation is supernatural, taking place from the inside out. The activities of reading the Bible and meditating on the Lord form images inside of us. These are the first creations that the Holy Spirit uses in renewing our minds, by which He affects the transformation of our entire being. As we behold His glory, we are changed! We *become* what we *behold*! Unfortunately, the supernatural power

---

59. "Metamorphosis," *Merriam-Webster.com*, 2015, http://www.merriam-webster.com/dictionary/metamorphosis.

of transformation can work against us if we behold the wrong thing, such as pornography.

Sociologists have discovered that child molesters almost always have a history of viewing child pornography, and that everyone who struggles with sex addiction has a pornography problem. Pornography has a powerful hold on the lives of many Americans and is consistently listed as the number one problem among Christian men![60] What is seldom discussed is the source of pornography's power—the fact that it is image-based. A man can be a Christian and truly love the Lord, but if he beholds pornographic material, he will be compelled into shameful behaviors by supernatural forces. I have ministered to many Christian men in bondage to pornography, and, in every case, these men thought that they could handle the problem on their own. They underestimated the power of pornographic images.[61] Now there is scientific evidence that looking at pornography releases a chemical in the brain that compels behavior. Science now agrees with the Bible—we become what we behold.

Over the years, we've ministered to young women who struggle with anorexia. In every case, these girls were thin, sometimes *too* thin; but they told us that when they would look at themselves in the mirror, they would see a fat person. They were not fat, but they *saw* themselves as fat, and that inner image was so powerful that it would drive them to the behaviors of fasting and purging. This proves the point of our book. Our inner image is more powerful than our outer image.

60. Documenting this statement is beyond the scope of this book. However, any reader who doubts this claim is encouraged to do some research. The problem of pornography in our nation can hardly be overstated. It is a big problem because it is image-based, and images *always* drive behavior.
61. I recommend watching the *Conquer Series: The Battle Plan for Purity*, a 6-disc DVD series that explores the problem of pornography in depth. Visit www.conquerseries.com for more information.

The same problem applies to young people who lewd music videos featuring artists like Beyoncé, Lady Gaga, and Miley Cyrus. Parents who allow their teens to continually behold, or gaze upon, these images seem surprised when their kids start dressing and talking like these unfortunate role models. Many moms and dads have no clue how supernatural forces use these images to compel their children to adopt dress styles and behaviors that they never would have adopted on their own.

Tattoos have become a phenomenon in this generation of Americans. I'm not making any judgments on those who get a tattoo. I have a lot of friends who are deeply in love with Jesus who have tattoos. But I'm trying to make a point. Tattoos are expensive, and the process is painful. When I was growing up, only sailors had them. So where did all its popularity come from? I believe that the idea of getting a tattoo never would have entered our minds unless we had first beheld them on people we admire.

Words are powerful because they form images in our minds. Sometimes, pictures are even more powerful. A picture is worth a thousand words, because we can close our eyes and still behold the images we have gazed upon days or even years before.

However, Simply Behold, and You Will Become!

Bill Johnson tells the story of a man who noticed a two-man work crew laboring alongside a city street. One man would dig a hole, and the second man would come right behind him and fill it in. This cycle was repeated several times until the observer could no longer restrain himself. He approached the men and said, "I've been watching you guys work really hard for quite a while and have to tell you that I don't understand what you're doing. What's going on here? One of you digs a hole and the other fills it in. What's the point?" One of the workers paused, wiped his brow, and said, "Yeah, it must look strange. The truth is that we're normally a three-man crew, but the guy who plants the trees called in sick today."

Religion puts us to work digging holes and filling them in, and when we notice that all our labor is producing no change in the scenery, religion tells us to dig another hole and fill it in. We can work really hard at religious self-transformation, but if the guy who plants the trees isn't in the picture, what's the point? Metaphorically speaking, that "guy" is the Spirit of God.

Real transformation takes place from the inside out. It is totally supernatural—the work of the Holy Spirit. If we think we can change ourselves by self-effort and religious disciplines, we're just going to wear ourselves out. We become by simply beholding! Transformation is no more difficult than simply looking at yourself in a mirror. But it has to be the right mirror. The mirror in your bathroom can tell you what you need to do to improve your appearance, but the mirror in God's Word tells you what God has already done for you; and believing what you see in the mirror of God's Word has the power to transform you into that image. Read this powerful verse one more time:

> *We all, with unveiled face, beholding as in a mirror the glory of the Lord, are being transformed into the same image from glory to glory, just as by the Spirit of the Lord.*
>
> (2 Corinthians 3:18 NKJV)

So stop striving. "*Be still, and know that I am God*" (Psalm 46:10 KJV).

Growing in God-Given Imagination

Words are powerful because they evoke images. When you hear the word *monkey*, you don't think of the letters M-O-N-K-E-Y. You "see" a monkey. If I tell you that I own a black Labrador retriever, your mind would immediately form an image of what my dog looks like. However, I find that many believers don't see images when they hear or read the Word of God.

For example, the Bible tells us that we are God's children by adoption.

> For all who are being led by the Spirit of God, these are sons of God. For you have not received a spirit of slavery leading to fear again, but you have received a spirit of adoption as sons by which we cry out, "Abba! Father!" The Spirit Himself testifies with our spirit that we are children of God, and if children, heirs also, heirs of God and fellow heirs with Christ. (Romans 8:14–17)

When God's Word tells you that you are a son of God by adoption, you should allow the Holy Spirit to create images in your heart of exactly what that means. It means that you are very special. When a couple has a baby, they aren't able to choose its gender or looks. On the other hand, when a couple adopts a child, they choose a specific child. God has only one natural Son. All the rest of us were adopted, which means that we were specially chosen!

Elizabeth and I have two children. We have never adopted a child, but we have been to an animal shelter and adopted a pet. I remember going to the dog kennel. All the dogs were on "death row"; if they were not adopted, they'd be euthanized. I remember our joy in choosing one, knowing that we had literally saved it from death. I remember bringing it into our home and making it part of the family.

I like to imagine that that's how God chose me. I was a sinner, far from God. I, too, was on "death row," but God *adopted* me. He *chose* me and *saved* me. He brought me into His household to take care of me. Furthermore, I also like to think about this: When most people go to a kennel to adopt a pet, they want the cutest, smartest, liveliest one of the bunch. Human nature looks for the one that stands out above the rest. But God is different! God goes to the pound and chooses to adopt the least attractive, sickest dog there, even the one with only three legs! That would be me. If you think this metaphor is off, read what the apostle Paul wrote to the church at Corinth:

> *Brothers and sisters, look at what you were when God called you. Not many of you were wise in the way the world judges wisdom. Not many of you had great influence. Not many of you came from important families. But God chose the foolish things of the world to shame the wise, and he chose the weak things of the world to shame the strong. He chose what the world thinks is unimportant and what the world looks down on and thinks is nothing in order to destroy what the world thinks is important. God did this so that no one can brag in his presence.* (1 Corinthians 1:26–29 NCV)

I like to imagine God going to the "kennel" of sinners that is known as the human race, and finding nothing but people on death row. I love to think about His grace, which compels Him to save by adoption. What really blesses me, however, is realizing that His choice isn't based on our talent, intelligence, good looks, or family pedigree. For the most part, He delights in choosing the weak, the foolish, and those whom the world considers of no importance. So when I read that God "adopts" me, I set about imagining how it all happened in the unseen realm of the first creation. As I behold these images, the Holy Spirit works a grateful humility into my soul, and I feel so special! Thanksgiving gushes up within me, and I feel so close to the Lord. Those images have replaced my pride and ingratitude with humility and thanksgiving. I am transformed from the inside out.

Working the Works of Jesus

Let me conclude this chapter with some thoughts on how God can use the power of imagination to bring a revival of Holy Spirit power to the American church.

I was saved and baptized in a Southern Baptist church where we were taught that the gifts of Holy Spirit had passed away. But one day, I read this:

> *Truly, truly, I say to you, he who believes in Me, the works that I do, he will do also; and greater works than these he will do; because I go to the Father.* (John 14:12)

I remember working my way through this verse, looking for loopholes to explain the powerlessness of my Christian faith and to give me an excuse for not doing the works that Jesus did, but I found none. I knew that I believed in Jesus and that He had gone to the Father, so, according to this verse, I should be doing "*works.*" However, there were no "*works*" in my life; neither were there any in the church I was attending. I remember going to my pastor to ask him about it. His answer was a little lame. He said that the gifts of the Holy Spirit had passed away and that the "*greater works*" Jesus mentioned had to do with the privilege we now have of leading people to Christ because of His resurrection, which, at that point in Jesus' journey, had not taken place yet. So leading people to Christ was the "greater work" He referred to. (Are you rolling your eyes yet?)

I was a brand-new, baby Christian, so there was no way I was going to challenge his explanation; but his answer didn't satisfy me. I knew that something was missing in his interpretation of this promise from Jesus. There was a "power outage" in my life and in my church, and I knew that there had to be a reason. It would be awhile before I discovered what it was.

Here were my questions:

+ If Jesus needed the power of God to authenticate His message, what makes us think that we don't?

+ Why isn't God's church moving more in the realm of signs and wonders and a demonstration of the power of the gospel that Paul referred to? (See 1 Corinthians 2:4–5.)

+ What is holding us back?

Based on what we've been learning in this book, I am convinced that the problem is that we cannot or do not "see" ourselves doing signs and wonders. If we cannot first imagine ourselves healing the sick, raising the dead, and casting out devils, we won't ever see it happen. There's been no first creation. Until we have a vision, dream, or picture of ourselves moving in the power of God inside us, we're never going to see it happen outside of us. Indeed, Jesus explained that this was the secret to how He performed His miracles!

The Key to a Ministry of Miracles

Sometimes we fail to remember that Jesus came to earth and carried out His ministry as a *Man*. He never ceased being God, but He "emptied" Himself of some of His divine attributes in order to be incarnated as flesh.[62] He ministered on earth as a Man empowered by the Holy Spirit. He said, *"I can of mine own self do nothing"* (John 5:30 KJV).

If Jesus was operating His ministry on earth as God, He would have never made this statement! He was modeling life as a Man. Here in John 5, Jesus healed a man who had been paralyzed for thirty-eight years. The Jews were challenging Him about performing the miracle on the Sabbath day and making Himself equal with God. His response confirms the message of this book: All the miracles are second creations!

> [Jesus said,] *Truly, truly, I say to you, the Son can do nothing of Himself, unless it is something He sees the Father doing; for whatever the Father does, these things the Son also does in like manner. For as the Father loves the Son, and shows Him all things that He Himself is doing; and the Father will show Him greater works than these, so that you will marvel. For just as the Father raises the dead and gives them life, even so the Son also gives life to whom He wishes.* (John 5:19–21)

If you unpack this passage, you will notice a few things about how Jesus moved in miracles and provided us a model of how we can move in the miraculous. First, Jesus said that He could do nothing of Himself (neither can we)! Second, He said that the only things He could do were things that He "saw" the Father doing. What does this mean? It could mean only that Jesus "saw," within Himself an inner image of what the Father wanted to be done, and He acted on that impression. Third, whatever Jesus

---

62. The great mystery of the kenosis of Christ, by which He emptied Himself by laying aside His divine privileges and transcendent glory is described by the apostle Paul in Philippians 2:5–7. While the Son of God never ceased being God, He did limit Himself by becoming flesh.

saw the Father doing was a first creation; the things He did "*in like manner*" were second creations, or miracles. Fourth, because the Father loved the Son, He "showed" Him what He was about to do, and the Son acted on it. The bottom line is this: The miracles of Jesus were second creations; the first creations took place in His heart and mind, where He "saw" what the Father wanted to do through Him.

There is absolutely nothing in this passage that is beyond what you and I can do *if* we allow God access to our imaginations. Jesus promised us that if we believe, we will do the works that He did. (See John 14:12.) Here He teaches us that we can do these things the same way He did—by "seeing" what the Father is doing, or wants to do, and acting on it.

One day I was in Cracker Barrel restaurant, waiting to be seated, when an elderly lady inched her way through the crowd with a walker. Immediately, I knew that the Father God wanted me to pray for her. I could see myself doing it. I didn't overthink the impression but just acted on it. I put my hand on her hand and asked, "What is your name, dear?" She answered, "Sarah." I then asked, "Do you mind if I pray for you?" She looked at me with a sweet smile and said, "Oh, yes!" I prayed a simple prayer and felt the presence of God come upon us. I wish I could say she threw away her walker and ran around the restaurant shouting "I'm healed!" That didn't happen. But there was a definite impartation of healing power; she looked up afterward and said, "Oh, *thank you*; that feels so much *better*!" In that moment, I truly felt God's pleasure in my simple act of obedience; but, at the same time, I realized how many hundreds of times that I was not available to the Holy Spirit to use me as He wanted in a given situation. However, I'm learning, and that's a great way to live.

Transformation by Renewal of the Mind

And do not be conformed to this world, but be transformed by the renewing of your mind.   (Romans 12:2)

Transformation takes place from the inside out. We need to renew the inside of us before we can impact the world outside of us. When we learn how to imagine the implications of metaphors and concepts like adoption, and visualize what the promises of Jesus really mean to us today, we can use these same principles to apply every promise in the Bible to our lives. We can literally find our story in God's story, and imagine ourselves living our lives like Abraham, Moses, or David, knowing that God will deal graciously with us just as He did with them. The applications are endless. We just need to look into the right mirror.

We become what we behold. Transformation happens from the inside out.

8

THE MIRACLE OF
A LITTLE GIRL AT
THE BEACH

When we lived in St. Louis, Missouri, I had a weekly breakfast with several businessmen in our church, where I was sharing some of the powerful truths contained in this book, and encouraging them to use the power of God-given imagination.

One morning after breakfast, one of the men, Bill Broaddus, pulled me aside and said, "Pastor Ray, I've lived this!" The story he proceeded to tell me is a perfect example of the power of imagination and how dreams come true.

Bill and Kathy were both twenty years old when they married in July 1982, and they wanted to start their family soon afterward. But Kathy didn't get pregnant. After about a year, Kathy decided to check with her doctor to see if there was anything they could do to increase their success rate. In his own words, Bill said,

We didn't know this would be the beginning of what became an indescribable barrage of different doctors, medical tests, and procedures over the next eight years. We went from one specialist to another. We spent tens of thousands of dollars on various procedures and treatments, very little of which was covered by insurance. After eight years and thousands of dollars, we got a word from the doctors—*idiopathic*, which means "We have no idea of what's wrong with you." At the end of all this, the head specialist at Southern Illinois University School of Medicine in Springfield, Illinois, encouraged us to adopt, because "this isn't going to happen for you."

We hit a dead end. I thought about writing a book describing all our experiences and calling it *She Cries Softly Now*, referring to how we both had reached our emotional limits and how hope was virtually gone.

A short time later, Bill was watching *The Phil Donahue Show*. Again, in his own words, he said,

As a busy farmer, I watched little TV and never followed Phil Donahue. I just happened to come home one afternoon and flipped on the TV show. I walked past the TV and heard an interesting interview from my office, so I went back to hit the record button for Kat. Looking back, it was just God's timing, as I had heard about [an assisted reproductive] procedure that had been developed by two doctors, both of whom just happened to practice in St. Louis! Unfortunately, the procedure didn't work for us. However, doctors did finally find out what was wrong with Kathy: She was unable to produce any viable eggs. Another dead end.

Finally, nine years into their marriage, Bill and Kathy decided to try another procedure that involved using a surrogate donor's egg. Bill would still be the biological father, and Kathy would carry the baby to full term. After receiving prayer from a Spirit-filled woman who was mentoring them, they went through with the process, and Kathy became pregnant!

During the pregnancy, Bill and Kathy were growing in the Lord, but they were facing a tremendous amount of spiritual warfare. There were complications with the pregnancy, a condition known as preeclampsia, in which Kathy's body began to reject the baby as a foreign object.

The situation got so bad that the baby had to be delivered three weeks early. It was a little girl, whom they named Rachel Jeanette. But then came more heartbreak. The baby was not well, and heart surgery was required. The baby was six days old when she died. Kathy had been so sick after the delivery that she had not gotten a chance to hold the child even once.

Kathy's doctor was one of the two specialists Bill had seen on *The Phil Donahue Show* who had written a book about this new procedure. After the death of the child, he told Bill and Kathy to "take some time off, give yourselves a break, and then we can try the procedure again. But you two will never have children on your own...that would take a *miracle*."

You would think this would have been the end for them, but it wasn't. God began to encourage their hearts again.

> We went home and got refocused. I remember reading Habakkuk 2:2–3, which says "*write the vision and make it plain*" (NKJV) and also Romans 4:17, which says to call things that are not as though they are. My mom had always told me that a picture is worth a thousand words, and we had learned some business principles about imagery and the power of a dream.

Because of this, I was looking through different magazines and cutting out pictures of different things. That's when I came across a picture of a little girl standing on the edge of a beach with her daddy, looking out over the water. I didn't think a lot about it, except for the fact that it would be really cool to stand on the beach like that someday with my own little girl, so I cut it out and hung it on my office wall.

Holiday Inn advertisement from the July/August 1991 issue of Travel Holiday, *page 102. For in-color photo, see inside back cover.*

Bill and Kathy refocused. They poured their lives into their church and dedicated themselves to helping people. What they didn't know, what they could not possibly know, was that the power of the image Bill had cut out of the magazine was powerfully at work in the invisible realm! The picture from the magazine was their first creation.

The Miracle Baby

About sixteen months later, in January 1994, Bill got up one morning and found a card from Kathy taped to the bathroom mirror above the sink. It read, "I love you, and you are going to be a daddy!"

Kathy called her doctor with the news. The nurse was hysterical, shaking his head in disbelief, and unable to talk! This time around, Kathy carried the baby to full term, and a little girl was born. They named her Lita. After twelve years of frustration, heartbreak, tragedy, and tens of thousands of dollars spent, Bill and Kathy had their miracle!

You may be wondering what this amazing testimony has to do with the power of imagination. Here's the rest of the story.

In July of 1998, Bill and Kathy went to the beach with their little four-year-old daughter. Unbeknownst to Bill, Kathy snapped a picture of him and Lita standing on the seashore. When they got back from vacation, they got their photos from the trip developed, and one of them looked really familiar! Here is a picture of Bill and Lita standing on the seashore:

For in-color photo, see inside back cover.

Later, as Bill was looking through the vacation photos, he immediately recognized the similarity between the picture he had cut out of the magazine five years earlier and the picture Kathy had taken at the beach. When he found the magazine image and placed it next to the vacation picture, here's what he saw:

For in-color photos, see inside back cover.

The image of the picture they had been "beholding" had become a reality!

The Miracle Heard 'Round the World

This is one of the most amazing miracles I've ever seen, and the perfect example of the power of images and God-given imagination! I have had the privilege of sharing this story and these pictures around the world, and people's reactions are stunning. People gasp. People cry. People shake their heads in disbelief. One pastor cried out, "This can't be real!" But it was! Even Bill Broaddus himself did not understand the dynamic power of imagination that had gone to work in him when he'd put the picture on his wall.

The picture in the magazine had burned an image inside of Bill's heart because it was his heart's desire to hold the hand of his own little girl. The magazine picture was an expression of the *dream* in Bill's heart. Based on what we've learned in this book, it was a first creation, because the image in the picture matched the desire of their hearts. And Lita's birth was a second creation!

This miracle has been heard around the world. When I tell this amazing story, there are gasps of awestruck wonder and many tears of joy. There's nothing quite like being confronted by an undeniable miracle from the Lord!

The Message Beyond the Message

This story is a message in itself, but there is more. Now take a careful look again at these two images:

For in-color photos, see inside back cover.

When you compare the image from the magazine on the left and the picture from the vacation, their similarities are undeniable. The bathing suits, the position of their feet, and little girls' hairstyles are eerily similar; but also notice the interesting contrasts:

- In the photo from the magazine, the father and daughter are standing on the edge of a swimming pool; but in the family photo, they are standing on the edge of an ocean.

- In both images, the father is holding his daughter's hand; but in the family photo, she seems to be holding Dad's hand close to her heart.
- The bucket in the family photo is bigger than the bucket in the magazine photo.
- The flippers in the family photo are bigger than the flippers in the magazine photo.

These contrasts teach us that the reality of the second creation, what happened in real life, is even greater than what happened in the first creation, the image in the magazine! God goes beyond our God-given imaginations and dreams! As the Scripture says,

> *Now unto him that is able to do exceeding abundantly above all that we ask or think, according to the power that worketh in us, unto him be glory in the church by Christ Jesus throughout all ages, world without end. Amen.*
>
> (Ephesians 3:20–21 KJV)

Can't you hear God calling out to you right now?

He's saying, "Ask it!" "Think it!" "Dream it!" "Imagine it!"

Then God reminds you that, after you think you've exhausted the bigness of your request, He is able to do *"exceeding abundantly above all that we ask or think"*! Bigger buckets! Bigger flippers! Oceans instead of swimming pools! And God gets all the glory!

God Still Wasn't Finished!

Just as the Scriptures tell us, God wasn't through in Bill and Kathy's life! Lita's birth turned out to be just the firstfruits of more blessings to come. Bill and Kathy Broaddus went on to have two more children! Those once barren are now a family of five.

Bill and Kathy Broaddus with their three children.

Let us be clear. Only God can work a miracle and bring about second creations like this, but we have a part to play. God is waiting on *us* to do the work of the first creation. It's up to us to imagine, desire, envision, and dream!

Review the Scriptures below, and as you read them, allow God to reawaken the dreamer inside you!

Old Testament

That night the LORD appeared to Solomon in a dream, and God said, "What do you want? Ask, and I will give it to you!" (1 Kings 3:5 NLT)

Then Nathan said to David, "Do all that is in your heart, for God is with you." (1 Chronicles 17:2)

*Delight thyself also in the L*ORD*: and he shall give thee the desires of thine heart.* (Psalm 37:4 KJV)

How the king…shouts with joy because you give him victory. For you have given him his heart's desire; you have withheld nothing he requested. (Psalm 21:1–2 NLT)

[God] grants the desires of those who fear him. (Psalm 145:19 NLT)

New Testament

Therefore I say unto you, What things soever ye desire, when ye pray, believe that ye receive them, and ye shall have them. (Mark 11:24 KJV)

If you abide in Me, and My words abide in you, you will ask what you desire, and it shall be done for you. (John 15:7 NKJV)

You did not choose Me, but I chose you and appointed you that you should go and bear fruit, and that your fruit should remain, that whatever you ask of the Father in My name He may give you. (John 15:16 NKJV)

All these Scriptures are *invitations* to imagine and to dream and then to tell God what you want! As Bill Johnson says, "God has made Himself vulnerable to our dreams."[63]

Everything is created twice. God is waiting on you and me to do what only we can do so that He can do what only He can do—miracles!

It's time to start dreaming again!

---

63. Bill Johnson, *Dreaming with God.*

9

THE ACTIVATION OF YOUR IMAGINATION

The gift of God-given imagination is the power within us to transform the world around us. But it must be *activated* in the invisible realm of first creations for it to work. So how do we do it?

Seven Practical Disciplines to Activate God-Given Imagination

Here are seven practical disciplines for the activation of your God-given imagination.

1. Stop, get quiet, and take a good, long, honest look at your life.

Embrace the realization that the principles in this book have *already* been at work in your life, whether you realize it or not. Recognize that what is inside of you has *already* been at work; it has created the world around you. You have been living out your entire life according to the images, or self-image, within you. Whatever's inside you has been determining your choices and your decisions, even up to this very moment. So how's that working out for you?

Begin now to accept personal responsibility for your life. Stop blaming God or others for your quality of life. Choose to accept responsibility for your present situation, and accept that you can change it for the better. Repent. Change your mind. Get to the heart of things.

When we first moved to Nashville, we bought a lovely home that had a wonderful deck on the back of the house. One day I was heading out the door onto the deck and noticed a spiderweb in the frame. Instinctively, I wiped it away and went about my business. The next day, the spiderweb was back! Again, I just wiped it away. Guess what? On the third day, it was back again, but this time, I heard a still, small voice inside of me saying, *Stop dealing with the cobwebs. Kill the spider!* So this time, after wiping away the cobwebs, I sprayed insecticide all around the door frame. That was the last time I had to deal with the cobwebs!

I have never forgotten this lesson from the Holy Spirit about life. So many of us spend our days trying to wipe away the cobwebs of daily life instead of dealing with the spider, which is the cause of the problem. The "cobwebs" of life are the unwanted circumstances created by the "spider," or the images inside of us. Recognize that the way to a better life is not to wage war on your circumstances but to allow God to paint some new pictures inside of you. Rejoice that now you know where to begin.

2. Learn how to practice the presence of God in your life.

God-given vision, dreams, and imaginations will come in the presence of the Lord.

When you read your Bible, especially the promises of God, let the words form images inside of you. Learn to find your story in God's story. When Jesus says, *"These signs shall follow them that believe"* (Mark 16:17 KJV), realize that He is talking about you! Begin to "see" yourself laying hands on the sick, prophesying, and casting out devils. (See Mark 16:17–18.)

When Jesus says that those who believe will do the same works He does (see John 14:12), lay hold of that promise. Begin to *imagine* yourself doing the works of Jesus. Get a vision of ministering to people as He did.

Our church offers training in supernatural ministry from the curriculum created by Pastor Bill Johnson's Bethel Church in Redding, California. Most people take Bible school courses and go to seminary in order to build their knowledge, but this school, in contrast, is about impartation. The information and revelation in the teaching is tremendous, but the real value of this school is how it exposes people to a supernatural culture. As the Word is taught and testimonies of what God is doing with ordinary people are shared, people "catch it." The students begin to see themselves laying hands on the sick and ministering prophetic words to people in their everyday world. Then they begin to do it. We have been amazed to see believers from every conceivable age group and occupation move into supernatural ministry because they began to believe they could. What would happen if every Christian in America began to imagine that they could do the works of Jesus? I believe we would see the next Great Awakening.

Remember that if you don't see it on the inside, you'll never see it on the outside. The reason most Christians aren't moving in the realm of the supernatural is simply because they can't see themselves moving in the realm of the supernatural.

When you sit quietly in God's presence, allow the Holy Spirit to help you imagine your preferred future. Allow yourself to dream of things that may seem impossible, and learn to bask in the vision of what God wants to do with you and through you. When you go through your workday, discipline yourself to practice the presence of God as often as you can. This is not as difficult as you may think.

> *In all your ways acknowledge Him, and He shall direct your paths.* (Proverbs 3:6 NKJV)

Jesus promised us that He would send the Holy Spirit, who would abide with us forever (see John 14:16); that He and the Father would make their *"abode"* (John 14:23 KJV) with those who love Him; that He would be with us *"always"* (Matthew 28:20 KJV). God is always present with us; He is *"closer than a brother"* (Proverbs 18:24 KJV) and *"a very present help in trouble"* (Psalm 46:1 KJV). The problem is not His lack of presence; it is our failure to acknowledge His presence!

Have you ever walked into a roomful of people where no one looked at you or spoke to you? You were present but your presence was not acknowledged. How did it make you feel? Unimportant? Irrelevant? Insignificant? Or even dishonored? I think God must feel this way. God is always in the room with you. He is always *present.* He is Immanuel, which means *"God with us"* (Matthew 1:23 KJV). He said He would never leave us or forsake us. (See Hebrews 13:5.) He is always there, but how often during the day do we truly acknowledge Him? What does this mean? Why do we do it? Here's how the dictionary defines *acknowledge:*

Acknowledge: to admit to be real or true; recognize the existence, truth, or fact of; to show or express recognition or realization of; to recognize the authority, validity, or claims of; to show or express appreciation or gratitude for.

Acknowledging God in all your ways is as simple as turning or inclining your heart toward Him, like a spiritual "nod." We can begin now to form the habit of conscious recognition of His presence, His authority, and His great love for us. It is simply practicing an awareness of His "there-ness." Be sensitive to the indwelling presence of the Holy Spirit and His ability to show you what He wants to do in your life.

When asked how He did His miracles, Jesus said, "I do only what I see the Father doing." (See John 5:19.) In other words, Jesus lived in the presence. The Father would show Him on the inside what He was doing or wanted to do on the outside. By this, we understand that all the miracles of Jesus were second creations!

As you go through your daily routine, practicing His presence, God will show you things. When we acknowledge Him in all our ways, He will direct our paths. (See Proverbs 3:6.) Thoughts, ideas, and images will float into our minds. Don't discount them. Give some weight to these impressions. Stop thinking of yourself as a physical being having a spiritual experience; instead, think of yourself as a spiritual being having a physical experience! Those little feelings, thoughts, and fleeting impressions are so often God's *"still small voice"* (1 Kings 19:12), giving you an inner image of what He wants to do through you.

3. Get in touch with your true self—your true identity in Christ.

Recognize and celebrate the knowledge that God knew you and wrote your name in His Book of Life *"before the foundation of the world"* (Ephesians 1:4 KJV; see also Revelation 17:8); He formed you in your mother's womb (see Psalm 139:13); He knows your every thought before you think it, and every word you speak before you speak it (see Psalm 139:4); He knows where you will go before you go, where you will lie down when you lie down, and is intimately acquainted with all your ways (see Psalm 139:3). You were saved by grace, a new creation in Christ Jesus, for a special purpose God had in mind for you from the beginning. (See 2 Timothy 1:9; 1 Corinthians 5:7.) If all this is true, why not trust Him to give you dreams, visions, and imaginations of the amazing things He wants do in your life?

Your daydreams, your deepest wishes and desires, come from Him. So dare to dream!

4. Cultivate inner images and pictures in your mind of your preferred future.

Write the vision and make it plain on tablets.
                                        (Habakkuk 2:2 NKJV)

The Broaddus family's miracle in chapter 8 was stunningly detailed in its fulfillment. If you can find a picture of your dream, clip it out and put it where you will see it every day. Or it may be good to write it down. Be specific. Don't just ask God for a dog. Tell Him what kind, color, and size of dog. Imagine what you want. Put images to your desires and your dreams. Life outside the kingdom will tell you not to get your hopes up, but God calls us to a faith that moves mountains.

I have ministered to people who come forward for altar calls in church services for over forty years. Occasionally, my conversation with one of these individuals goes something like this:

"How can I pray for you?"

"I have an unspoken request."

The first time this happened, I was caught so flat-footed, I almost laughed. (Fortunately, I didn't.) I want to be gracious here, but come on—how would I know how to pray for something unspoken? I got in the habit of handling this by just praying a generalized prayer asking for God's blessing on that person's life. However, I don't do that anymore because I think it encourages people to approach God in a very impersonal way that dishonors Him. For example, if you ask one of your beloved children what you might do for him, and he replies, "I have an unspoken need," what would you say to him? To go to God with an unspoken request is just religious nonsense.

Remember that everything is created twice. Our prayer request is really the first creation that comes out of the unseen realm of our hopes, desires, and dreams of our preferred future. The answer to that prayer is the second creation. But if the first creation of our prayer request is unclear and unspecified, the second creation of the answered prayer in the visible world may be so unclear and unspecified that we don't even recognize it when it happens.

Take the time to do the proper work of the first creation. Don't take your dream to God until it's clear in your own mind. Be specific. The prophet Habakkuk said, *"Write the vision and make it plain"* (Habakkuk 2:2 NKJV). Then, when God answers the prayer, you'll recognize the answer when it comes!

5. Guard your dream.

A pregnant woman takes special care to protect the new life growing inside her. We need to have the same attitude about the hopes and dreams that are incubating inside us.[64]

Cultivate relationships with people who will encourage you. Stay away from those who won't. People will trample your dreams. Joseph was doing fine until he shared his dreams with his half brothers! (See Genesis 37.) If David had listened to his brother and Saul, he never would have fought Goliath. (See 1 Samuel 17:28–37.)

Thirty years ago, I began to imagine that the Lord wanted the people in the Bible study I'd been leading as a businessman to become a local church. One particular couple had been so faithful in attendance and had a wonderful gift of serving the group in general. We shared with them the seed of the vision that was forming in our hearts, and they were very encouraging. One day, the man called me for lunch. I was happy for the opportunity to fellowship with him, and walked into our meeting without a negative thought in my mind. However, after the meal, he took on a very serious tone and said, "You know we love you, and you have a great teaching gift, but we've decided to move on. The truth is that we just don't see this thing going anywhere." He might as well have hit me in the stomach. I was totally deflated. We had really been counting on this couple to be a mainstay for us in moving forward, so this was a big blow; but thank God it wasn't fatal. We didn't allow their decision and judgment of things to kill the dream. They did leave, but we held on.

---

64. For guidance in this area, I recommend reading Dr. Mark Chironna's book *Obtaining a Harvest from Your Seed of Dreams.*

The Bible study became a church; and, seventeen years later, we passed the baton—a church property with a strong congregation and facilities that were appraised for over seven million dollars—to a new leader. All we'd had when we started the Bible study was a metal music stand we used as a pulpit and a tape recorder from Radio Shack, a one hundred-dollar investment. The couple that left at that point went on to join the staff of another great church in the city where they'd served for many years. They weren't bad people; they were great people. But there was a moment when they almost doused our dream.

Over the years, I've told this story to many dreamers who had become discouraged when the people they'd been counting on had abandoned them. Folks will let you down, but hold on to your dream! God wants you to count on Him, not on people. People will come and go in and out of your life. But your dream has the power to keep you on course, if you don't give up.

Recognize that you live in a fallen world designed for discouragement. Immersing yourself in the news and politics of the day may make you downsize your dreams or give up on them altogether, so be sensitive to allowing too much negativism into your soul. Most of the news of the day is *bad* news, and it's easy to let your mind be flooded with facts that can frustrate you or even make you angry. The world tends to work in such a way that discourages dreamers, but...

"If the dream is big enough, the facts don't matter."
—Mark Chironna

While we must guard ourselves from allowing the bad news of the day to overwhelm us, we also need to remember that Christ came to transform every dimension of human life, not just our "religious" life. God wants to use us to affect the world around us, so we need to be informed about what's going on. The ostrich is a large bird that can't fly, known for burying its head in the sand when it senses danger. We can't be "ostrich" Christians, living in denial of the dangers around us. Refusing to acknowledge the dangers of our world doesn't remove us from them.

We live in a culture saturated with Greek dualism, a philosophy that conceptually divides life into two opposed or contrasted aspects. Dualistic thinking draws a sharp distinction between the physical world and the spiritual (or mental) world, seeing them as separate and unrelated. Unfortunately, many of God's people unconsciously subscribe to this compartmentalization of life, which sees obviously spiritual exercises such as going to church, praying, and reading the Bible as separate and disconnected from the "real" world of daily living. This is why some Christians go to church on Sunday but still live pretty much like the rest of the world Monday through Saturday. This is why so many Christians ignorantly accept the faulty notion of the separation of church and state, in which religion is banished from engagement in everything from politics to public schools.

We need to recognize that Christ came to influence *every* dimension of life, and He intended His kingdom to leaven *every* level of human experience in our culture. (See Matthew 13:33.) Indeed, God wants to give His people dreams and imaginations that provide answers and solutions for the problems reflected of the day. So when the days seem to get darker, the opportunities to spread the good news of the kingdom get bigger! Don't let the negativism of the world dampen your dreams. On the other hand, be informed. Remember that Jesus came to do more than just solve the sin problem. He came to solve all problems. He came to change the world!

Some of God's greatest dreams of changing the world through us will come to us when things seem to be getting worse. Man's extremity is God's opportunity. Remember that very great advancement in human history came because someone dreamed that things could be better. One of my favorite quotes on our subject comes from Robert F. Kennedy:

> "There are those who look at things the way they are, and ask why? I dream of things that never were, and ask why not?"
> —Robert F. Kennedy

Don't be afraid to look at things that are and wonder *Why?* But don't stop there. Start dreaming of things that could be and ask yourself, *Why not?*

6. Dress for success.

Years ago, we hired a church consultant to spend a weekend with us and do a comprehensive evaluation of our ministry functions on Sunday for an objective, professional viewpoint. We learned a lot from his report, but one thing that he told us especially stuck with me: "If you are a small church that wants to be a larger church, you have to start acting like a larger church *now*."

Acting out the future you want in the present you have is a powerful way to activate your imagination. Dress now for the success to come. The consultant's counsel resonated with me because it reconnected me with a principle that I had learned in my twenty years of being a sales manager in the business world. Start shaping your personal image *now* to match where you want to go. John T. Molloy's classic business book *Dress for Success* was required reading for all the sales teams I led. Originally published in 1975, this best seller has been published in many editions as styles have changed over the years, but the relevance of the theme has never changed: "Don't dress for where you are. Dress for where you are going."[65]

Molloy addresses the importance of the image you project to others. For example, if I see a man get out of his car dressed in tennis shoes, tennis shorts, and carrying a tennis racket, I would assume he is on his way to play tennis. If I see a man dressed in a coat and tie gassing up his car at 9 AM on Sunday morning, I would assume he is on his way to church. The point is that, in the "real" world, people instinctively understand a principle often overlooked by the "church" world—image is important.

"Dress for success. Image is very important. People judge you by the way you look on the outside."
—*Brian Tracy*

The way you see yourself on the inside subconsciously dictates the level of your personal grooming and clothing choices. When your inner image gets an upgrade, your outward image, how you project yourself to others, ought to get a commensurate upgrade.

65. John T. Molloy, *Dress for Success* (New York, NY: Warner Books, 1975).

I realize that some of you may be struggling with this point. Whenever I touch on this subject in sermons, resistance arises. Some folks even seek to correct me, often quoting the verse in which God instructs the prophet Samuel to lay hands on the young shepherd boy David:

> But the LORD said to Samuel, "Do not look at [David's brother Eliab's] appearance or at his physical stature, because I have refused him. For the Lord does not see as man sees; for man looks at the outward appearance, but the LORD looks at the heart."....And Samuel said to Jesse, "Are all the young men here?" Then he said, "There remains yet the youngest, and there he is, keeping the sheep." And Samuel said to Jesse, "Send and bring him. For we will not sit down till he comes here." So he sent and brought him in. Now he was ruddy, with bright eyes, and good-looking. And the LORD said, "Arise, anoint him; for this is the one!"
>
> (1 Samuel 16:7, 11–12 NKJV)

When I stress the importance of how you dress and the image you present to others, well-meaning people sometimes feel compelled to remind me that the outward appearance doesn't matter to God, because He looks at the heart. Of course He does; but the rest of the verse is also true! "...man looks at the outward appearance."

When I go before the Lord, I know He is looking at my heart; but when I go before men, I know they are looking at my outward appearance! If all men were like God, appearance wouldn't matter; but, unfortunately, we are dealing with men most of the time. The image we present to others really does affect how they judge us.

While I'm on the subject, let me go a little bit farther. Twenty years ago, a big question in the American church was whether it was okay to wear jeans to church. I was in a large city where one of the churches had purchased large, expensive billboards with the headline "Jeans are OK with us!" all over town. I remember thinking at the time, *With all the trouble we have in the world, and how much people need to hear the gospel of the kingdom, why is this the issue people want to spend all this money on to address?* The truth is, of course, jeans are all right to wear to church. I often preach in jeans, and I've never cared that much about what people wear to church, as long as their clothing is not blatantly immodest. However, those who think that God does not care about our clothing and outer image or that godly people of the Bible didn't care how they looked or what their outer appearance signaled are ignorant of the Scriptures. For example:

+ God spends a great deal of time regarding how His priests were to clothe themselves. (See, for example, Exodus 28.)

+ When Joseph was delivered from prison, he shaved himself and changed his clothes before appearing in front of Pharaoh. (See Genesis 41:14.)

+ The Lord heard the prayers of repentant kings who had clothed themselves in sackcloth and ashes. (See 2 Kings 19:1; 1 Chronicles 21:16, 28.)

+ Godly Mordecai and other Jews put on sackcloth before the Lord. (See Esther 4:1–4.)

+ Esther's appearance before the king caused him to look on her with favor. (See Esther 5:1–2.)

+ A royal daughter mentioned in the Psalms wore special garments. (See Psalm 45:13.)

- A demon-possessed Gadarene who had been running around naked was delivered and later found in his right mind, clothed, and seated at the feet of Jesus. The change God made inside him was reflected on the outside. (See Mark 5:15.)

- Jesus, in one parable, describes a king who kicks people out of the wedding feast because they showed disrespect by not wearing proper clothing. (See Matthew 22:11–13.)

- On judgment day, all of God's people will be wearing white robes—an outward reflection of their inner glorification! (See Revelation 7:9.)

If the president of the United States invited you to visit him in his office, would you think of showing up in a sweat suit? I don't think so. You would instinctively want to present yourself in a way that shows that you honor him and his high office. In the same way, if we *really* believe that our Sunday morning worship service means that we're going into the presence of the King of Kings and the Lord of Lords, wouldn't we be conscious of how we present ourselves to Him? Isn't God worthy of much more honor than the president of the United States—a mere man? Please don't get me wrong. I am not making a case for a Sunday-morning dress code; I am just pointing out that if we really understand what's happening in the Spirit in our Sunday-morning worship services, we will consider how we present ourselves before the Lord in outward appearance.

God looks at the heart, but He doesn't disregard grooming, either. Ditch the religious thinking and start bringing your outer self into harmony with your inner self. After all, if you're giving your inner image a makeover, you might as well do the same with your outer image.

7. Include love and service for others in your dreams and imagination.

As I travel around the country and awaken people to the power of their God-given imagination, one big question comes up over and over again: How can I really be sure that what I'm imagining and what I'm dreaming is in the will of God for my life?"

This is a great question. Unfortunately, there are no simple answers, but there are some principles and guidelines that can help us discern whether an image or dream is within the will of God. One of the most important guidelines deserves an entire chapter of its own:

> *But the greatest among you shall be your servant.*
>
> (Matthew 23:11)

SERVING THE
PURPOSE OF GOD
IN YOUR GENERATION

*For David, after he had served the purpose of God in his
own generation, fell asleep.*
—Acts 13:36

An epitaph is something written on a person's tombstone. Over the years, I've collected some of the more humorous epitaphs in the world.

The tombstone of famous comedian W. C. Fields:

I'd rather be in Philadelphia.

On the tombstone of a lawyer in England:

John Strange
Here lies an honest lawyer
And that is Strange.

A tombstone in Thurmont, Maryland, reads:

Here lies an Atheist,
All dressed up with no place to go.

And my favorite is from a cemetery in Georgia; on the tombstone of B. P. Roberts is inscribed, "I TOLD YOU I WAS SICK."

Men can write whatever they like on their tombstones, and some may make us smile; but what should really make us sit up and pay attention is when God writes an epitaph. In Acts 13:36, the Holy Spirit records His testimony regarding the life of Israel's greatest king, David, who *"served the purpose of God in his own generation."*

I have often pondered this verse and prayed that God's testimony of my life would resemble what He said about David. To discover God's purpose for our lives and to faithfully serve that purpose ought to be our top priorities.

What is the definition of the term *purpose?*

Purpose: the reason for which something exists or is done, made, used etc.; an intended or desired result; end; aim; goal.

We instinctively know that we are not on this earth by acci-
dent. Sooner or later, we come to realize that God chose our
place of birth and the time in which we were born into world history. We know that something deep inside us cries out for true
fulfillment in life and is motivating us to discover it. We know
that God knows our purpose, but we may not realize that God
expects us to seek it out.

> It is the glory of God to conceal a matter, but the glory of
> kings is to search out a matter.   (Proverbs 25:2 NKJV)

Discovering God's Purpose

In his classic book *In Pursuit of Purpose*, Myles Munroe
offered these words of wisdom: "Until purpose is discovered, existence has no meaning, for purpose is the source of fulfillment."[66]

King David discovered and served the purpose of God in
his lifetime. The purpose of this book is to awaken the dreamer
inside you. Whenever a serious Christian begins to activate
their God-given imagination and dream about what their preferred future might look like, the same nagging questions always
emerge: "How do I know if what I want is what God wants?"
"How can I know if what I am dreaming is really God's will for
me?"

These are great questions. These are important questions. In
previous chapters, I've given some biblical guidelines for testing
the legitimacy of what we desire, dream, and imagine. Most of
these checks have to do with our motivation: *"You ask and do not
receive, because you ask with wrong motives, so that you may spend
it on your pleasures"* (James 4:3).

---

66. Myles Munroe, *In Pursuit of Purpose* (Shippensburg, PA: Destiny Image
Publishers, 1992), 1.

The word *pleasures* in this verse comes from the Greek word for lust. The English word *lust* is almost always used in a negative context to express intense desire or craving for something personally pleasurable. Lusts are powerful because they are always accompanied by imaginations. If a Christian man begins to dream and fantasize about having an affair with his neighbor's wife, we can be sure that the Holy Spirit will convict him of it as sin. Other desires we have, however, may not be so obviously unbiblical. Is it wrong to strongly desire, imagine, and pray for a vacation to Hawaii? Is it OK to ask God for a much-needed new car?

Too many of God's people are double-minded when it comes to using the power of their God-given imagination because they fear acting outside of God's will, especially when it comes to matters of personal blessing.

So is there a great master key we can use when we are seeking the purpose of God for our lives and testing the legitimacy of our hopes, dreams, and imaginations? The answer is yes, there is! Always keep in mind that finding and serving the purpose of God involves a motivation to love and serve others!

The Only Way to Truly Serve God

In 1975, I went to work for Ted L. Snider, a Christian businessman in Little Rock, Arkansas, who would have a powerful influence on the rest of my life. Ted had hired me to manage his outdoor advertising business, one of several advertising/communications companies he owned. Ted was Southern Baptist and a wonderful family man. He loved the Lord, but he never came across as *religious*. He had the most wonderful way of treating his people and running his companies on Christian principles, which he would communicate in the most practical ways.

Ted is one of the finest Christians I've ever known, and I could fill a small book with the wisdom I'd gained during the six years I worked for him. A couple of those life lessons went deep into my soul and remain to this day.

Ted believed that the only way we can really serve God is by serving others. How can we really say we that serve God? How can we serve Someone who has no needs? God has no needs, but people have a lot of needs, and God loves people. So the only way we can really serve God is by serving people. This simple philosophy permeated everything we did in every division of Snider Corporation. The idea of serving people was behind his acquisition of several radio stations, a statewide news network, a Muzak (background music) franchise, a travel agency, and an outdoor advertising division, in which I served. Ted was successful in everything he did, and everyone admired him as a successful businessman. Most people never knew that his primary motivation was not to make money—it was to serve people. The money followed.

In retrospect, I realize that Ted was a dreamer. He imagined some great things, and they all came to pass. His dreams were safeguarded by his primary motivation to service others. We can learn a lesson from Ted's story. The secret to fulfillment, happiness, and even greatness lies in the heart that loves to serve and help people solve their problems. When that spirit is working within us, we can trust our dreams.

The Key to Greatness and Happiness

Answer these two questions for me: Do you want to be great? Do you want to be happy?

The first question can be somewhat difficult for Christians to answer, but the second is a no-brainer. Everyone wants to be happy. Jesus promised us that both greatness and happiness are not only possible but guaranteed to those who live their lives in love and service to others.

Take the matter of "greatness." When Jesus' disciples came to Him asking for promotion and greatness, He did not rebuke them for wanting to be great, but He did challenge them to consider their motives.

> *And whoever wants to be greatest of all must be the slave of all. For even I, the Messiah, am not here to be served, but to help others, and to give my life as a ransom for many.*
> (Mark 10:44–45 TLB)

Greatness comes by serving others! And once we are sure that our hearts are resolved to love and serve others, we can let our dreams and imaginations run wild. There is so much need out there and so many hurting people in this world; but instead of looking at all the problems, start imagining how you can be a solution! There is none greater than Jesus, and He said that He did not come to *be* served but to serve! (See Matthew 20:28.) There is nothing more Christ-like than loving people by serving and helping them. This will come to us naturally once we get a much-needed deliverance from self-centeredness.

> *Whoever finds their life will lose it, and whoever loses their life for my sake will find it.*   (Matthew 10:39 NIV)

The Abrahamic prototype

Abraham is the "*father of all them that believe*" (Romans 4:11 KJV), and we are to "*walk in the steps of that faith*" (Romans 4:12 KJV). Since Abraham is a prototype, or model, for all believers, we should pay careful attention to what God said to him.

*And I will make you a great nation, and I will bless you,
and make your name great; and so you shall be a blessing.*
(Genesis 12:2)

God promised that He would bless Abraham. We all want
God's blessing, but many times we overlook that God's purpose
for blessing Abraham was so that he could be a blessing! God
saves us so that we can live like Jesus, which means serving others
and being a blessing to people everywhere we go. When this revelation hits your soul, it will transform your life and move you
to find and fulfill God's purpose for you in this generation. This
is your pathway to true happiness and fulfillment. In his classic
book *The Purpose Driven Life: What on Earth Am I Here For?*,
Rick Warren expresses this concept perfectly:

> You were put on earth to make a contribution. You weren't
> created just to consume resources—to eat, breathe, and
> take up space. God designed you to make a difference with
> your life....You were created to add to life on earth, not just
> take from it. God wants you to give something back.[67]

There are so many unhappy people in this world.
Unfortunately, too many of them are Christians. If only we could
lay hold of Jesus' simple solution to the problem. Napoleon Hill
offers an excellent paraphrase of Jesus' prescription for those
seeking happiness.

> You are seeking happiness. Learn this lesson, once and
> forever, that you will find happiness only by helping others
> find it![68]

---

67. Rick Warren, *The Purpose Driven Life: What on Earth Am I Here For?*
(Grand Rapids, MI: Zondervan, 2002), Day 29.
68. Napoleon Hill, *Outwitting the Devil: The Secret to Freedom and Success*
(Sharon Lechter, 2011), 13.

Matthew Barnett and the Dream Center

Matthew Barnett is the son of Tommy Barnett, the long-time pastor of one of America's greatest churches. In his book *The Cause Within You: Finding the One Great Thing You Were Created to Do in This World*, Matthew tells the amazing story of how his famous Dream Center ministry began. Matthew had gone to the inner city of Los Angeles to build a great church, but after a few weeks, the small congregation he had inherited dwindled down to zero! Discouraged and feeling like a failure, Matthew wept out loud the Sunday morning when no one showed up to church. But God interrupted his pity party.

> At that moment I heard God speak to me... I did not bring you here to build a great church. I brought you here to build people—these people. You build the people. I'll build the church.[69]

This was Matthew's wake-up call. God wasn't done. Matthew said that the Lord went on to say this:

> I don't ever want you to talk or even think about "success" again. Think about being a blessing. Success is obedience to your calling; I have called you to bless these people. Love them. Heal them. Help them. Serve them.[70]

That was the great turning point for Matthew's life and ministry, a work that has brought salvation, healing, and deliverance to thousands and helped transform the inner city of Los Angeles. I wish every Christian everywhere would read Matthew's book, because it perfectly captures the essence of God's purpose for

69. Matthew Barnett, *The Cause Within You: Finding the One Great Thing You Were Created to Do in This World* (Carol Stream, IL: Tyndale House Publishers, 2011), 13.
70. Ibid.

our lives—to "find a need and fill it."[71] In it, Matthew sums up what he learned about helping and serving people—how it is the key to fulfillment in life. Here's what he shares:

+ Everyone has a God-given cause designed specifically for him or her.

+ God's cause for your life is easier to fulfill than your self-designed cause.

+ When you find it, your true cause will liberate your passion and gifts.

+ God's cause for you relates to helping and serving people.

+ The best time to figure out the cause within you is now.[72]

There has never been a better time for a Holy Spirit outpouring of God-given imaginations and dreams than now.

The Time Is Now!

The world is hurting. Multitudes have never heard the gospel. Even those of us who live in the greatest, most prosperous nation on earth face problems that seem insurmountable. However, man's extremity is God's opportunity. The fulfillment of the prophecy for the last days is at hand...

> "And it shall be in the last days," God says, "That I will pour forth of My Spirit upon all mankind; and your sons and your daughters shall **prophesy**, and your young men shall see **visions**, and your old men shall dream **dreams**; even on My bondslaves, both men and women, I will in those days

71. Ibid., 156.
72. Ibid., 51.

*pour forth of My Spirit and they shall **prophesy**."*

(Acts 2:17–18)

God is pouring out His Spirit upon sons, daughters, young and old men, and all mankind! Signs of this outpouring will be visions, dreams, and God-given imaginations that release the power within you to change the world around you. And it all begins when you are willing to do the work of first creation by connecting with your deepest hopes and dreams to create your own future. If your heart is full of love for God and a desire to serve people, you can trust the Lord to direct your thoughts.

So "let the river run, let all the dreamers wake the nation. Come, the New Jerusalem!"[73]

---

73. Carly Simon, "Let the River Run," 1992.

ABOUT THE AUTHOR

Ray W. McCollum has always known how to dream. As a child, he imagined himself as a baseball radio announcer. By his teens and twenties, he had absorbed an understanding of imagination's power from secular business books like *Think and Grow Rich* by Napoleon Hill and *As a Man Thinketh* by James Allen. Ray used these principles to build a successful business career in radio broadcasting and advertising. But in Little Rock, Arkansas, in 1971 at the age of twenty-seven, Ray came to Christ. After his conversion, Ray dedicated himself to learning and teaching the Bible as a Christian layman. The more he learned, the more he realized that many of the secular books about the power of imagination that had so impacted his life actually had a biblical basis. He discovered again and again that the world had basically "hijacked" these truths from the Word of God. (And mostly without giving God any credit!)

In 1981, the McCollum family relocated to Nashville, Tennessee, where Ray owned an outdoor advertising company.

His gift for Bible teaching attracted so many followers that he began to seek the Lord about whether he was being called to the ministry. He had a successful company, and he enjoyed the work, but Ray also had a secret dream of teaching the Bible full-time. The idea of planting a church was very exciting to him, but starting a church from scratch carried no financial guarantees—and he had a mortgage, a business loan, and two children in high school. As he agonized over which direction to take, the Lord said to him very clearly, "Why don't you sell everything you have and just trust Me?" So he did. He sold his company. He sold his house. He sold his car and paid cash for a smaller one. And in 1986, at age forty-two, he launched what eventually became Bethel World Outreach Center in Brentwood, Tennessee, a suburb of Nashville.

The Bethel World Outreach Center began as a Bible study with a $100-investment in a metal music stand "pulpit" from the Baptist bookstore and a tape recorder from Radio Shack. When the study became a little church, it purchased a small chapel in south Nashville for $75,000. In 1988, the church relocated to a larger building and five acres of land in Brentwood. When he passed the leadership along in 2000, the congregation was strong and healthy and the property was appraised for over $7 million. The biggest dream of Ray's life thus far had come true!

After several years of itinerant ministry and a five-year pastorate in Austin, Texas, Ray returned to Brentwood to plant a new church with his son, Todd, who is now lead pastor of Celebration Church. While Ray is still actively involved in the local church, he spends much time writing and traveling. His passion today, at age seventy-one, is to invest in the next generation. As he says it, "I want to give as much as I can, to as many as I can, for as long as I can."

FOR MORE BY
RAY MCCOLLUM...

Additional teaching materials available at www.pastorray.com.

Audiovisual seminar of "The Power of God-Given Imagination" is available on DVD or by download at www.pastorray.com.

Pastor Ray Bible School courses, audiovisual plus class notes, available for download:

101: *An Introduction to the Prophetic View of Scripture*

An amazing new way to understand the Bible! 12 sessions

201: *Genesis: The Book of Beginnings*

Understand Genesis, and you unlock the whole Bible. 12 sessions.

301: *Kingdom Nation*

The Kingdom of God is the central subject of the entire Bible. 12 sessions.

401: *Pastor Ray's Preaching School*

Do you want to teach and preach the Bible effectively? Here's how! 12 sessions.

501: *Discovering Your Identity in Christ*

You are not who you think you are. You are who God says you are! 8 sessions.

601: *The Panorama of Redemption*

An exhaustive presentation of New Testament Christian life, prefigured in the Old Testament Exodus of Israel. 12 sessions.

For free sermons by Pastor Ray, visit www.ccnashville.com.

For a free video of Session 4 of the "Imagination" Seminar, visit www.pastorray.com.

To connect on Facebook, look up Ray McCollum, Nashville, Tennessee or Pastor Ray's Bible School.

Welcome to Our House!

We Have a Special Gift for You

It is our privilege and pleasure to share in your love of Christian books. We are committed to bringing you authors and books that feed, challenge, and enrich your faith.

To show our appreciation, we invite you to sign up to receive a specially selected **Reader Appreciation Gift**, with our compliments. Just go to the Web address at the bottom of this page.

God bless you as you seek a deeper walk with Him!

WE HAVE A GIFT FOR YOU. VISIT:

whpub.me/nonfictionthx

WHITAKER
HOUSE